Published by: Kansas City Star Books
1729 Grand Blvd.
Kansas City, Missouri, USA 64108

First edition, first printing
ISBN: 978-1-61169-044-6

Library of Congress Control Number:
2009924512

Printed in the United States of America by Walsworth Publishing Co., Marceline, Missouri

To order copies, call toll-free 866-834-7467.

www.PickleDish.com
www.PickleDishStore.com

My Stars VII

Patterns from The Kansas City Star • Volume VII

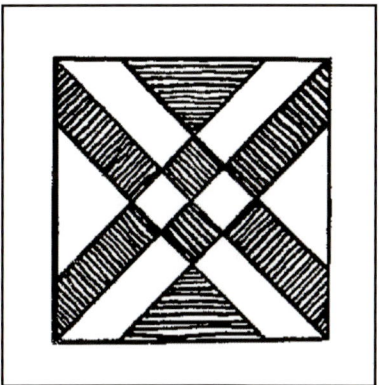

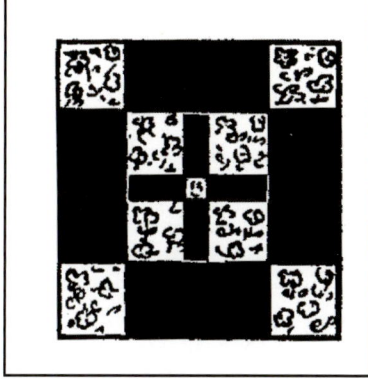

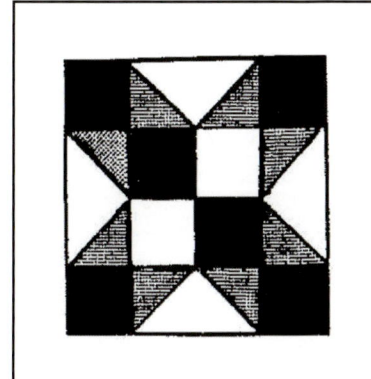
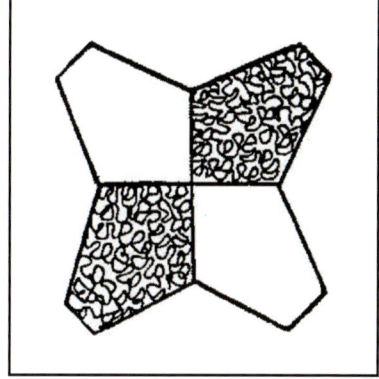
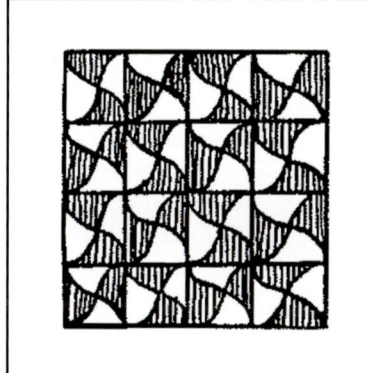

INTRODUCTION

Welcome to the seventh book in our *My Stars* series – we're trucking right along! The books are going to be such great collector's items once we get them all completed.

It's fun offering these patterns in a random order because there is sure to be something for everyone in each book. Patterns in this book include Broken Stone, Indian Star, Ozark Trail, Queen Charlotte's Crown and Mountain Road, just to name a few.

Be sure to check out the photographs of the gorgeous quilts that accompany some of the blocks. The quilt contributors are people just like you – fans of the historical patterns who enjoy making new quilts with historical blocks. It's always exciting to see a new twist!

The Kansas City Star began printing traditional quilt patterns in 1928. The patterns were a weekly feature in The Star or its sister publications, *The Weekly Star* and the *Star Farmer*, from 1928 until the mid-1930s, then less regularly until 1961. By the time the last one ran, more than 1,000 had been published in the papers, which circulated in seven Midwestern states as well as North Carolina, Kentucky and Texas.

The *My Stars* series is Kansas City Star Quilts' effort to redraft the entire historical collection, and offer it in bound printed volumes for pattern lovers to stitch and collect. Each of the 25 patterns in this book includes fabric requirements, templates and assembly instructions, as well as the original sketch and caption that were printed in the newspaper. Sit back and enjoy the heritage of quilting with the seventh installment.

-Diane McLendon, editor

*　　*　　*

ACKNOWLEDGEMENTS

I would like to thank the wonderful team that has made My Star Collection and the *My Stars* series possible:
Edie McGinnis, Kim Walsh, Jane Miller, Doug Weaver, Aaron Leimkuehler, Jo Ann Groves,
and of course, our quilt friends who have graciously provided their quilts to be included in this book.

-Diane McLendon, editor

*　　*　　*

My Star Collection is a weekly subscription service where subscribers download a pdf pattern – from The Kansas City Star's historical 1928 to 1961 collection – each week. The subscription is for a year of patterns – 52 in all. For more information or to sign up, visit subscriptions.pickledish.com.

TABLE OF CONTENTS

Broken Stone

Block Size: 6" finished

Fabric Needed

Dark blue

Blue and tan print

Cream and blue print

You'll need templates for this block.

Cutting Instructions

From the cream and blue fabric, cut

1 piece using template B

From the blue and tan print fabric, cut

4 pieces using template A

From the dark blue fabric, cut

4 pieces using template C

To Make the Block

1 Sew the dark blue C pieces to the tan/blue print A pieces.

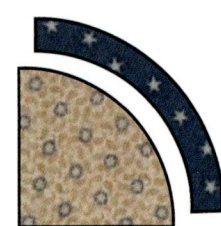

2 Sew the A/C pieces to the center B piece to complete the block.

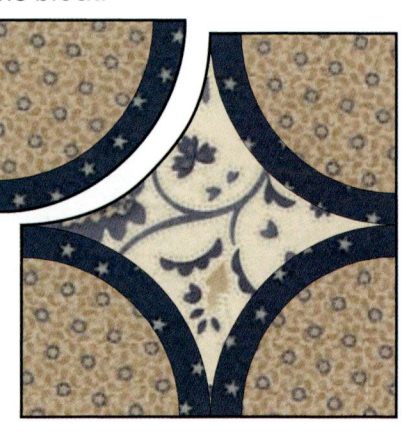

Broken Stone

From The Kansas City Star,

September 2, 1933:

No. 321

Original size - 8 3/4"

This pattern was sent to The Star by a quilt fan who says that the entire quilt is made of these blocks which form a beautiful design when the quilt is finished. She suggests a solid color and a figured material for best results. Thank you, Mrs. O. W. Lowman.

History of the Block

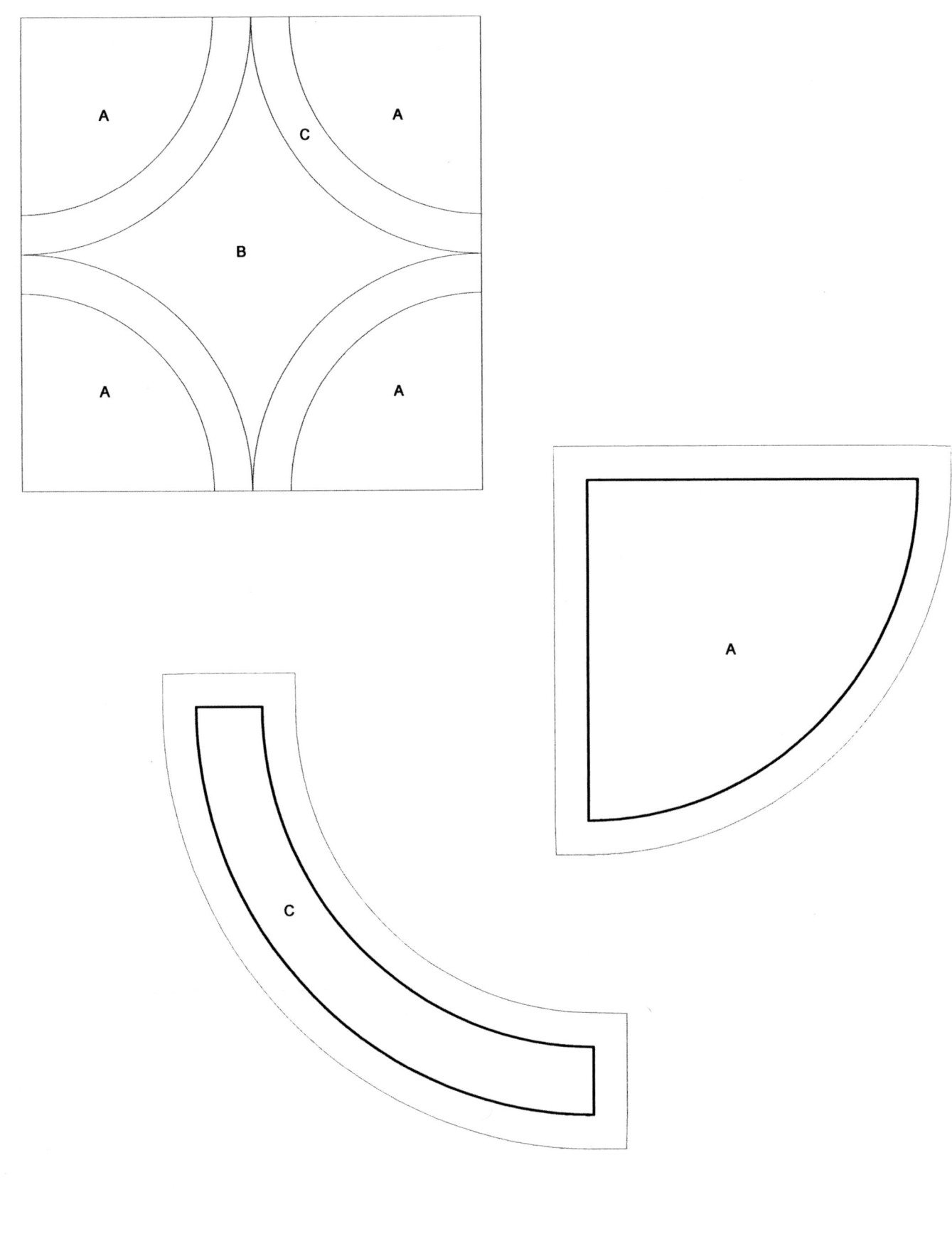

Broken Stone

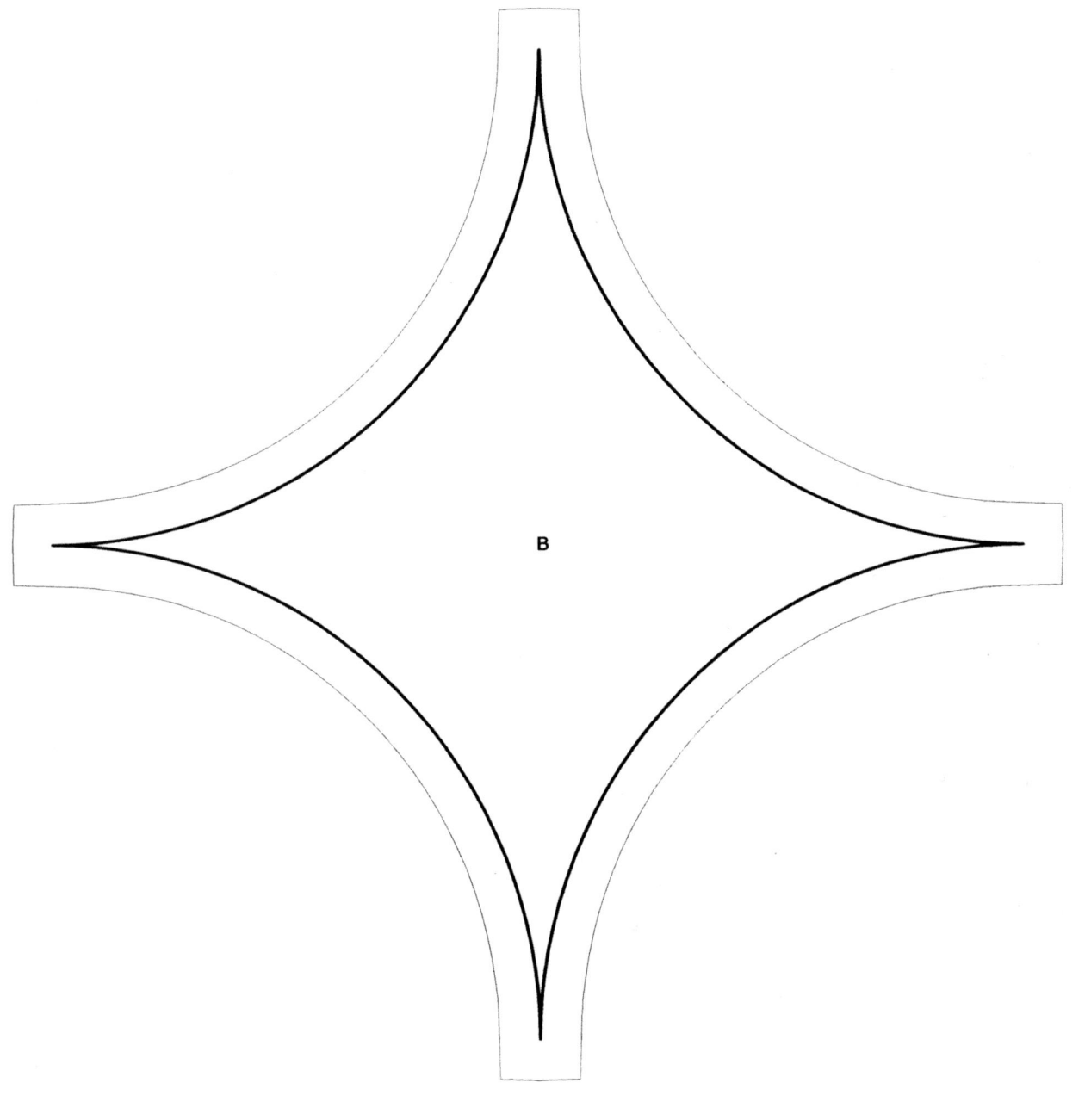

B

Template

Appeared in The Star **August 21, 1935**

Railroad Crossing

Railroad Crossing

Block Size: 12" finished

Fabric Needed

Red

Cream

Note: If you are cutting your pieces using the rotary cutting instructions, you will need to use a scant quarter-inch seam allowance when sewing.

Cutting Instructions

From the cream-colored fabric, cut

1 – 8 1/4" square. Cut the square from corner to corner twice on the diagonal or cut 4 triangles using template B.

4 – 1 5/8" x 5 3/8" rectangles (template C).

From the red fabric, cut

8 – 1 5/8" x 5 3/8" rectangles (template C).

1 – 4" square (template D).

2 – 3 3/8" squares. Cut the squares from corner to corner once on the diagonal or cut 4 triangles using template A.

To Make the Block

1 Sew the C rectangles together as shown. Make 4.

2 Sew a cream B triangle to either side of two of the rectangle units.

3 Sew a rectangle unit to either side of the center square.

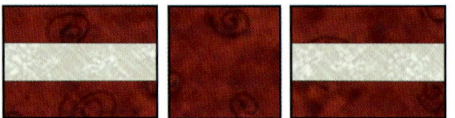

4 Sew the three units together as shown.

5 Add the A triangles to the four corners to complete the block.

From The Kansas City Star,

August 21, 1935:

No. 415

Original size – 10 1/2"

Here is a quilt which many quilt fans call a "straight line quilt," as it has no curved seams. It is a striking quilt in prints with a plain color of the same tone.

Railroad Crossing

Template

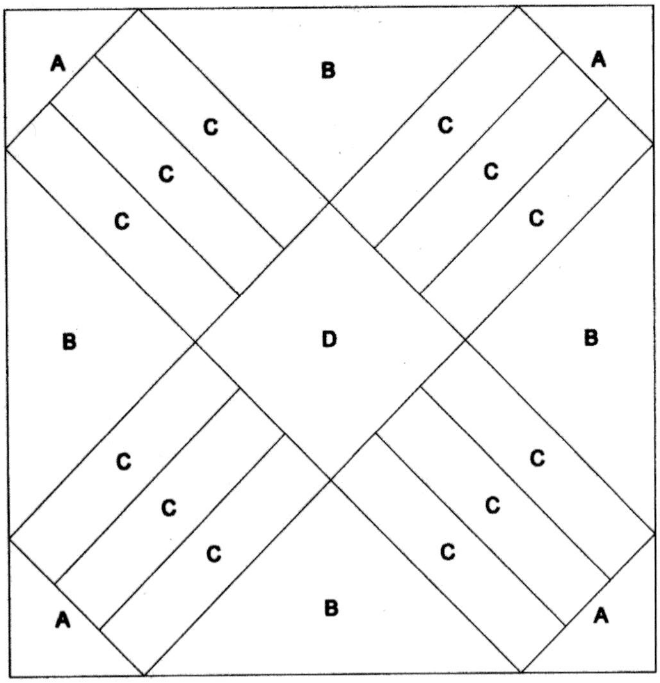
A
B
A
C
C
C
C
C
C
B
D
B
C
C
C
C
C
C
A
B
A

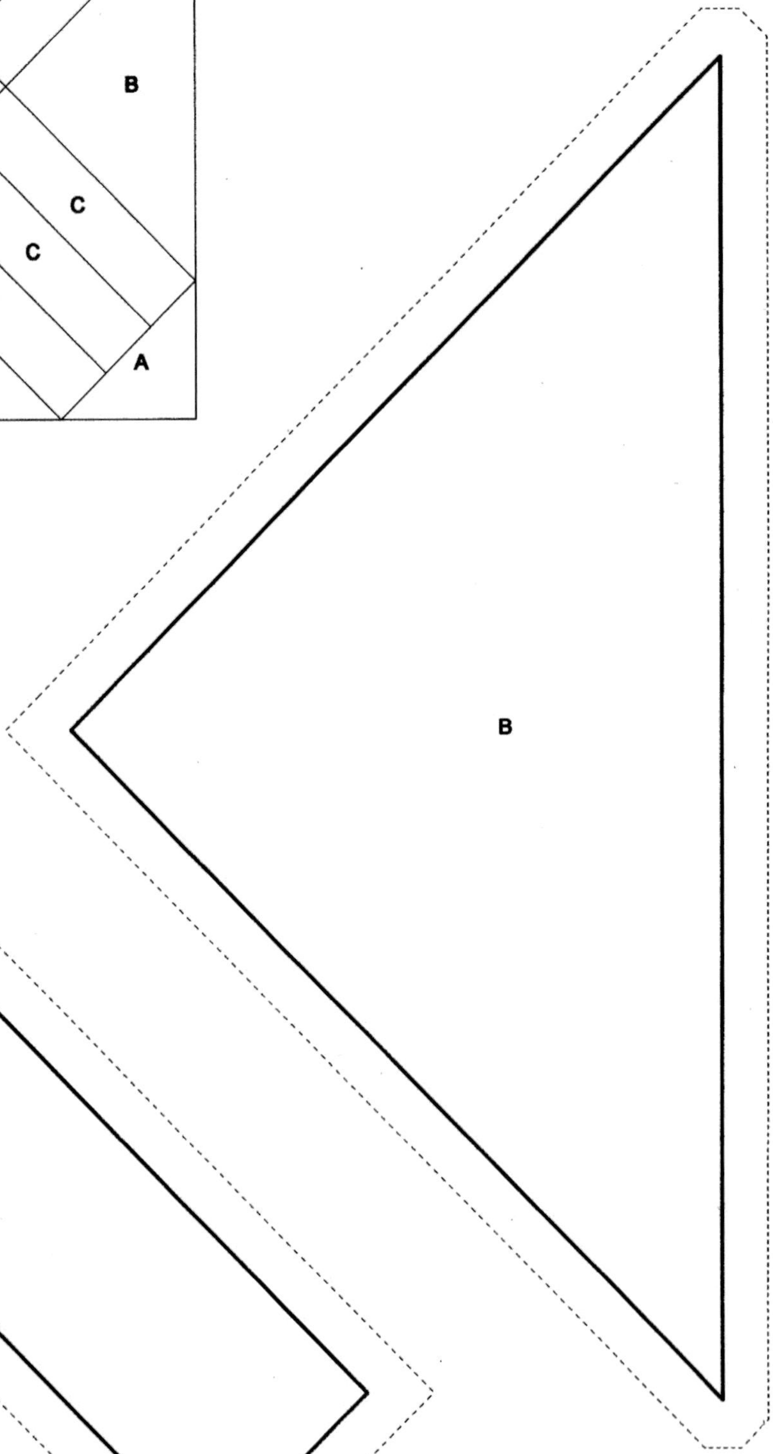
B

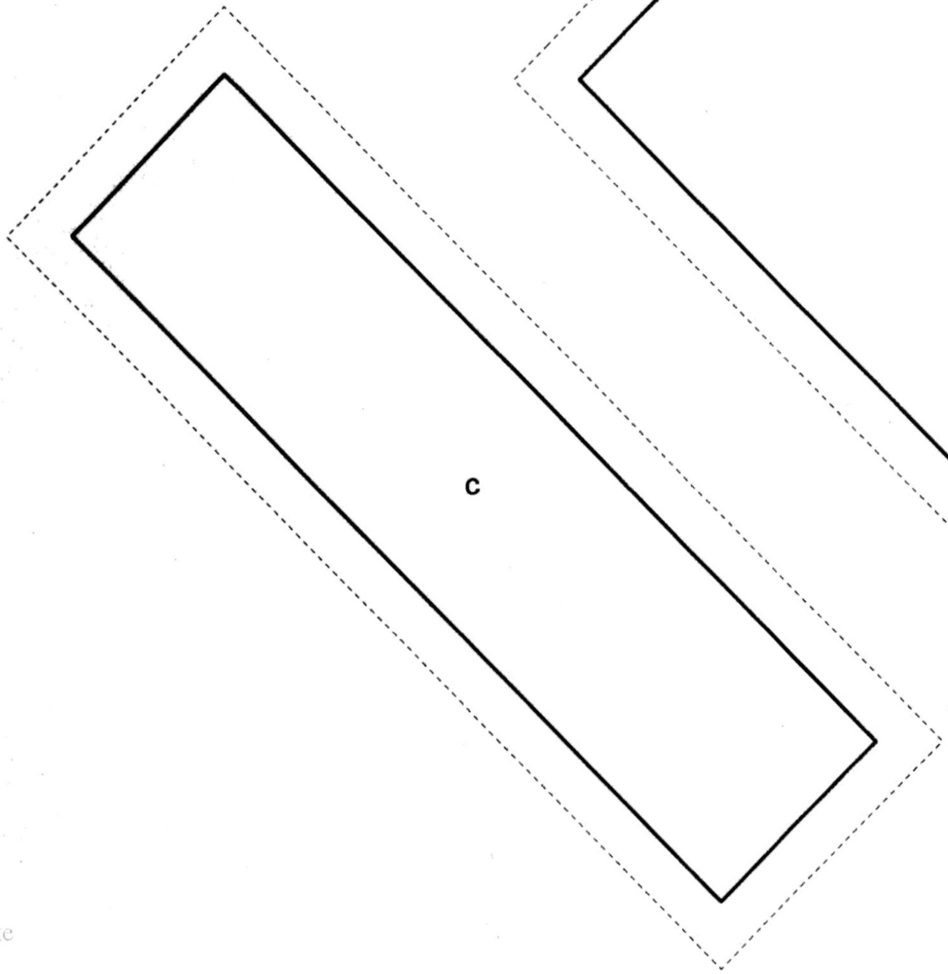
C

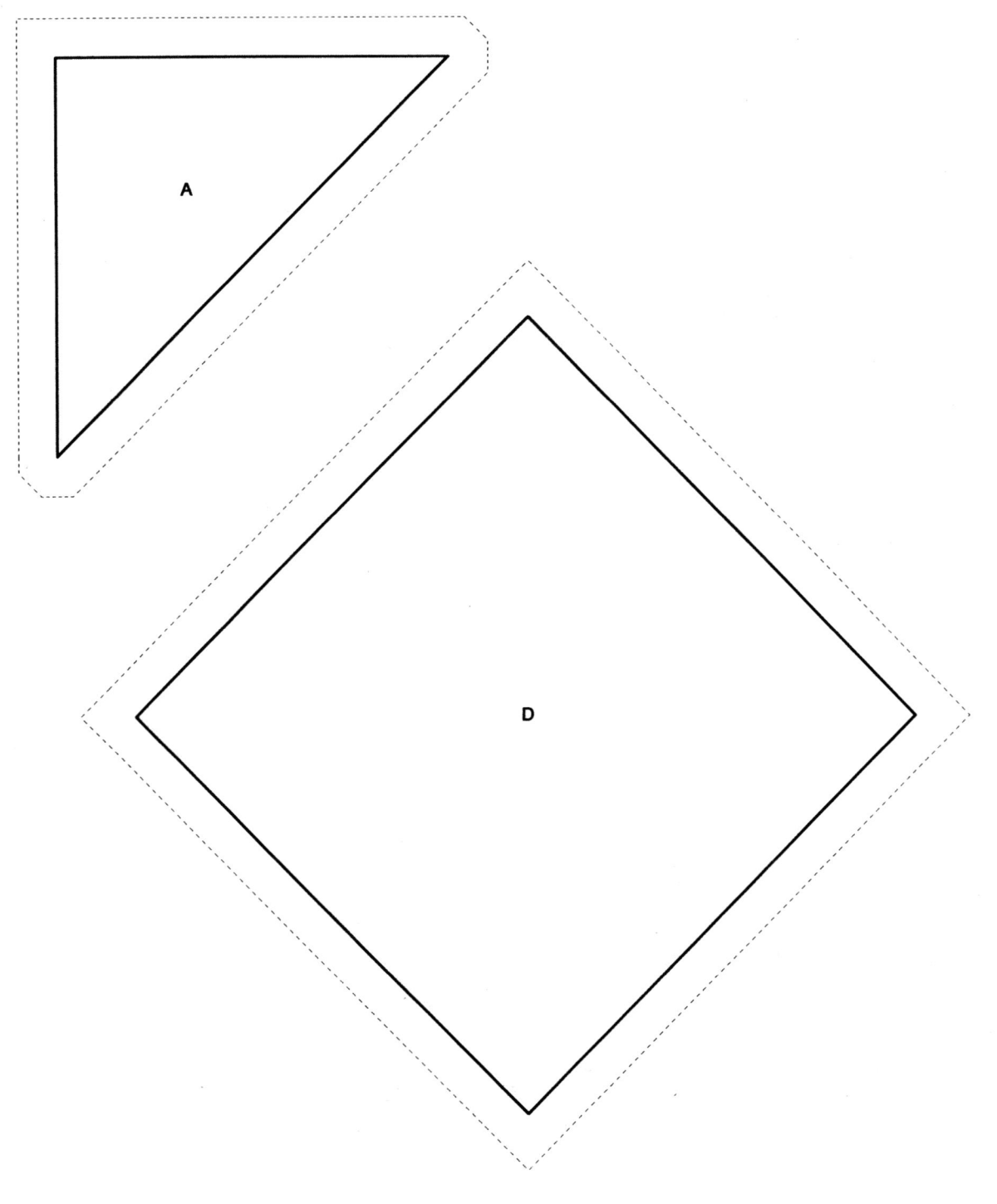

A

D

Template

Appeared in The Star **March, 26, 1941**

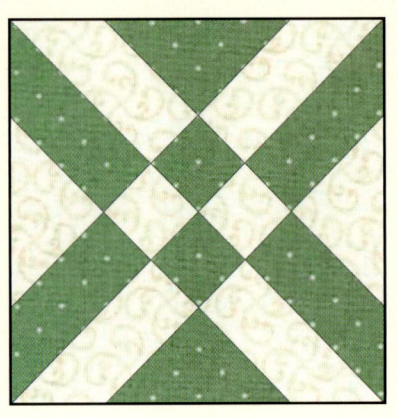

Arrowhead

Block Size: 12" finished

Fabric Needed

Green print

Cream

You'll need templates for this block.

Cutting Instructions

From the cream fabric, cut

2 pieces using template A

2 pieces using template C

2 pieces using template B

2 pieces using template D

From the green print fabric, cut

2 pieces using template A

2 pieces using template C

2 pieces using template B

2 pieces using template D

To Make the Block

1

This block gets sewn together on the diagonal.

Sew a cream B piece to a green C piece. Add a cream A piece and end with a green B piece. Refer to the diagram below and make 2 of these units.

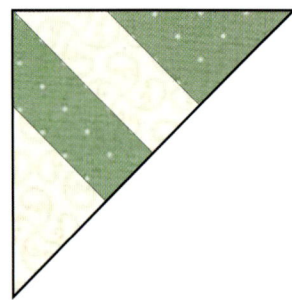

2

Now sew the four D squares together to make a 4-patch unit.

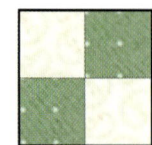

3

Sew a green A piece to a cream C piece. Make two then sew one to each side of the 4-patch.

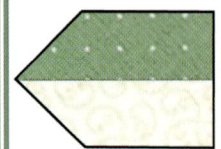

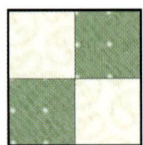

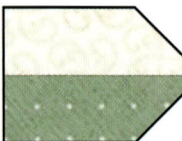

Arrowhead

4 Sew the three strips together to complete the block.

From The Kansas City Star,

March, 26, 1941:

No. 643

Original size – 10"

This pattern is a favorite with Mrs. F. J. Jordan, Fort Cobb, Ok. Sometimes she sets the blocks together with plain strips or plain squares, and again, she makes the entire top of arrowhead blocks seams.

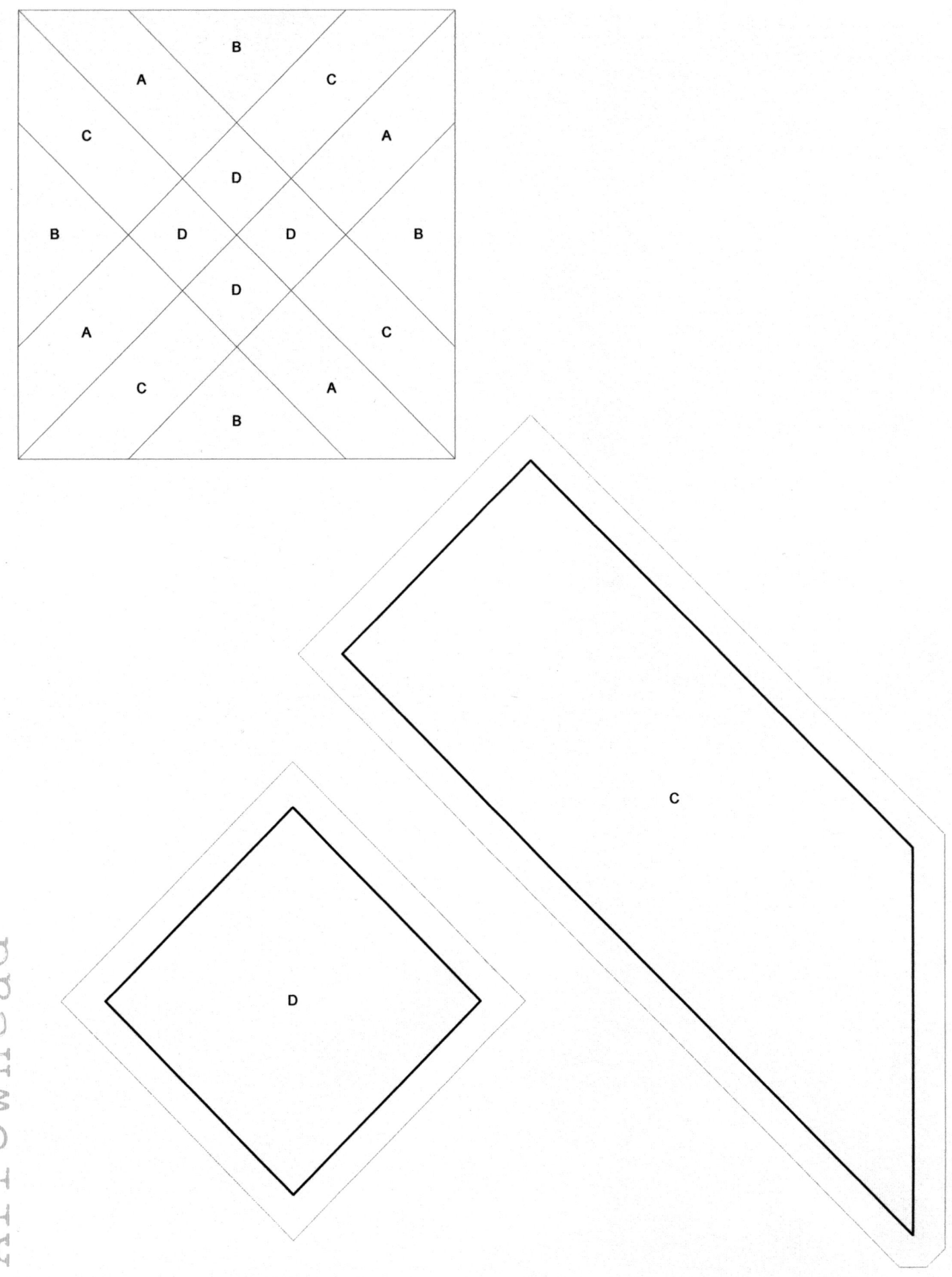

Arrowhead

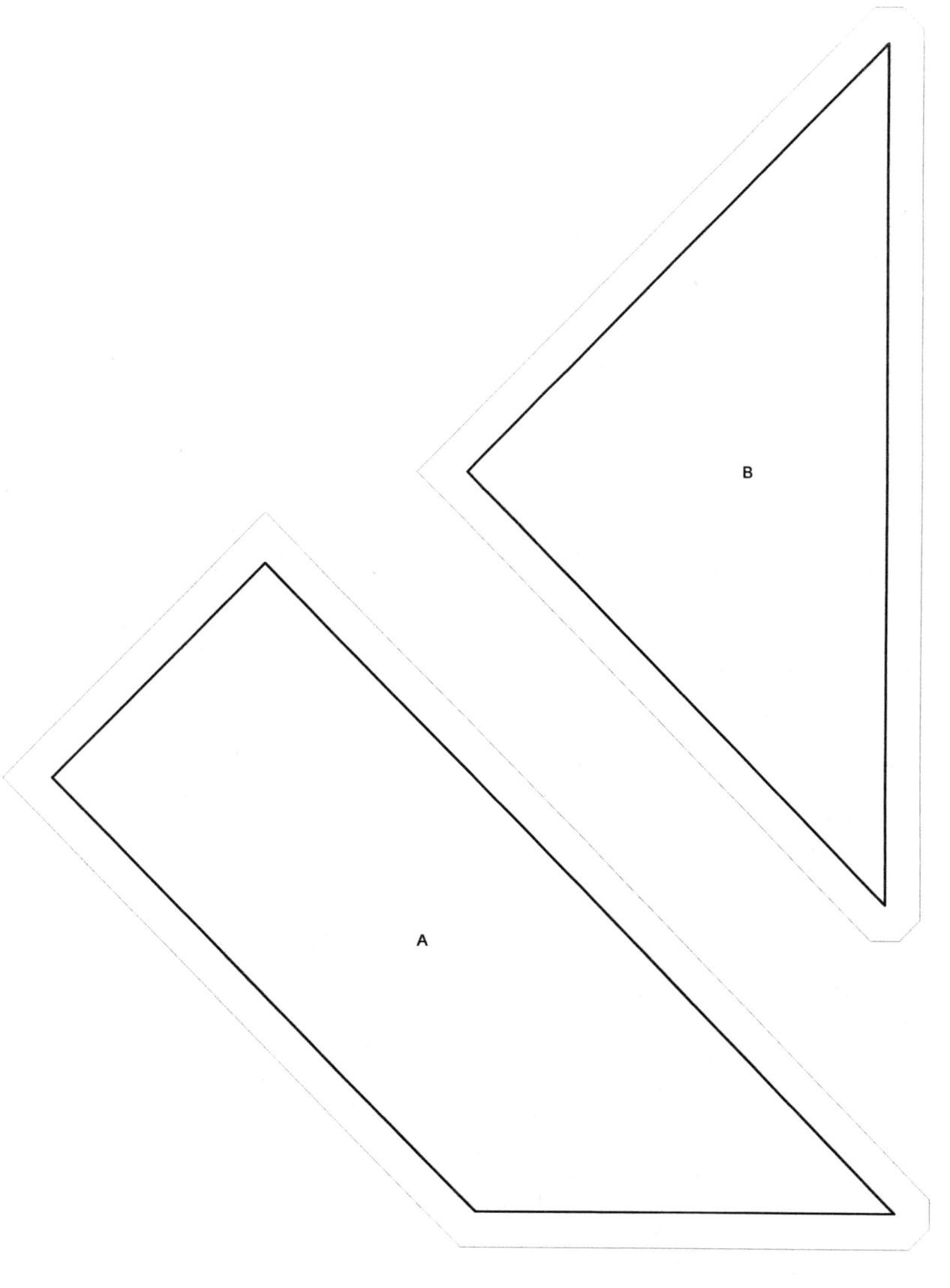

B

A

"Christmas in Vicksburg" designed by Linda M. Thielfoldt, Troy, Mich. and
quilted by Linda M. Thielfoldt, The Quilted Goose, Troy, Mich.

Appeared in The Star **March 9, 1935**

Bridle Path

Block Size: 12" finished

To Make the Block

1

You will need to make half-square triangle units for this block.

To make half-square triangles, draw a line from corner to corner on the diagonal on the reverse side of the lightest fabric. Place a light square atop a darker square and sew 1/4" on each side of the line. Use your rotary cutter and cut on the line. Open each unit and press toward the darkest fabric.

Make 8 dark red print/grey half-square triangles. Set aside.

2

Sew the pink/red print 1 1/2" squares and the grey 1 1/2" squares together to make 9-patch blocks. Make 4.

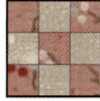

3

Sew the dark red print 1 1/2" squares and the grey 1 1/2" squares together to make 9-patch blocks. Make 4.

Fabric Needed

1 Dark red print

1 Pink/red print

1 Grey

You can use rotary cutting directions for this block. If you choose to use templates, they are provided as well.

Cutting Instructions

From the grey fabric, cut

4 – 3 7/8" squares or cut 8 triangles using template B

32 – 1 1/2" squares or use template A

From the dark red print, cut

4 – 3 7/8" squares or cut 8 triangles using template B

20 – 1 1/2" squares or use template A

From the pink/red print, cut

20 – 1 1/2" squares or use template A

Bridle Path

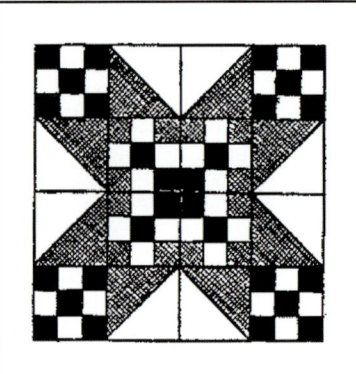

From The Kansas City Star,

March 9, 1935:

No. 392

Original size - 16"

These large blocks make an attractive quilt. The "path" is traced by the dark blocks. This quilt design was contributed by Gladys Simmons, Grand Pass, Mo.

4 Sew the half-square triangle units and the 9-patch units into rows as shown below.

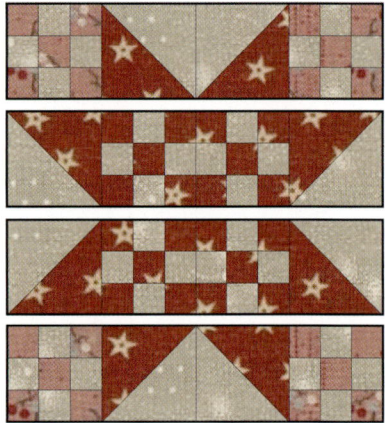

5 Sew the rows together to complete the block.

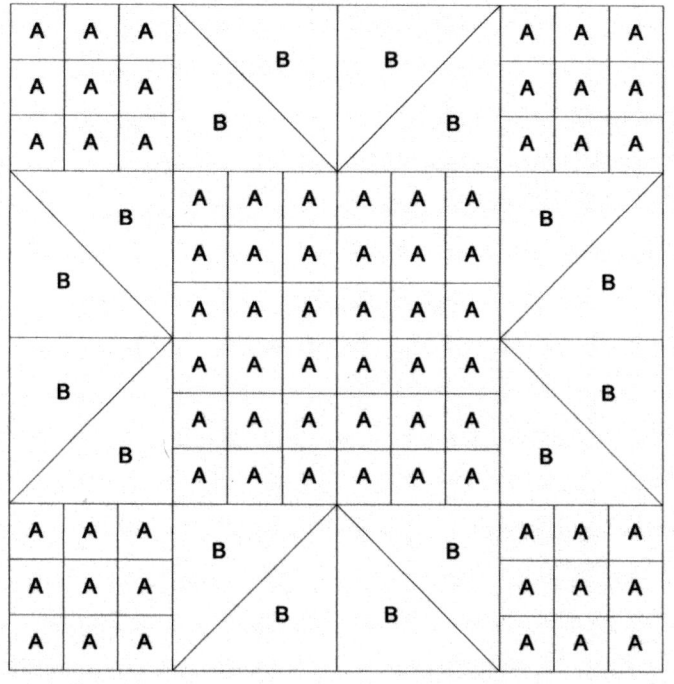

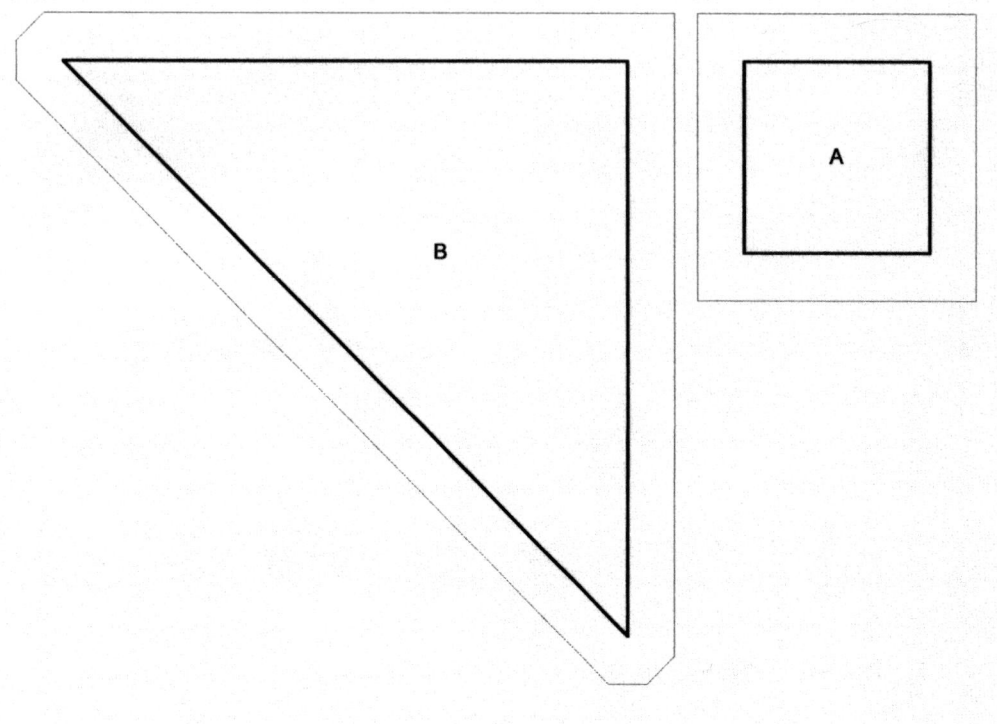

Bridle Path

First appeared in The Star **January 5, 1935**

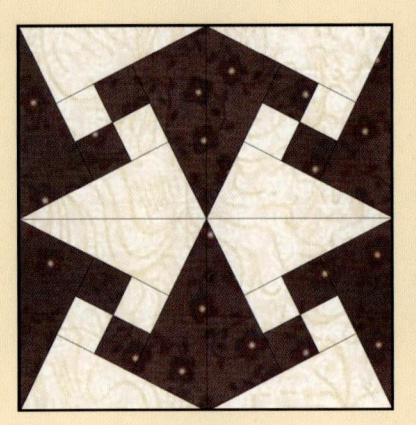

Arabic Lattice

Block Size: 12" finished

Fabric Needed

Brown

Cream

You'll need templates for this block.

Cutting Instructions

From the brown fabric, cut

4 pieces using template A

4 pieces using template B

8 squares using template C

From the cream fabric, cut

4 pieces using template A

4 pieces using template B

8 squares using template C

To Make the Block

1

Sew two cream C squares to two brown C squares to make a 4-patch units like the one shown below. Make 4.

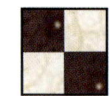

2

Sew a cream A piece to the center 4-patch unit. Notice that piece A extends past the 4-patch unit. On this first seam, you need to stop sewing when you reach the midway point of the second square. Leave the remainder of the seam open.

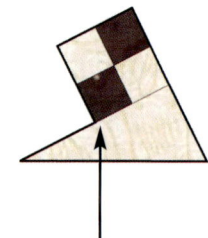

Stop sewing where shown.

3

Now add a brown A piece.

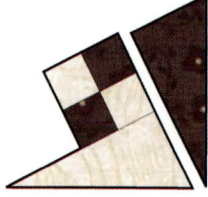

4

Now a cream A piece to the top.

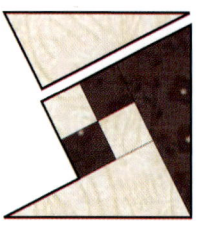

Arabic Lattice

5

Sew a brown A piece to the left side. Go back and close up the first seam line. This is one-fourth of the block. Make 2.

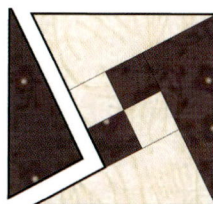

6

Using the same technique as above, make two quadrants of the block using the brown and cream B pieces around the 4-patch unit.

7

Sew the four quadrants together as shown to complete the block.

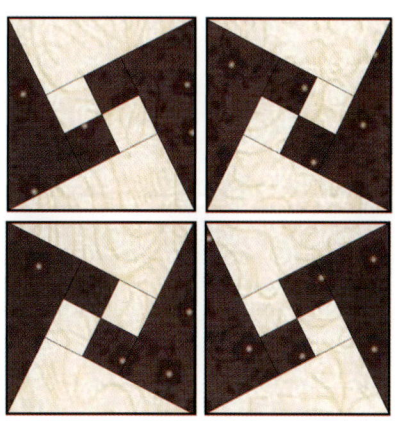

From The Kansas City Star, January 5, 1935:

No. 384

Original size – 5 1/2"

This quilt pattern is simple in the individual units as you see, but gives the impression of an intricate pattern when set together. Allow for seams.

March 27, 1935:

No. 394

Original size – 5 1/2"

This odd pattern is repeated by request. The individual blocks are simple. Allow for seams.

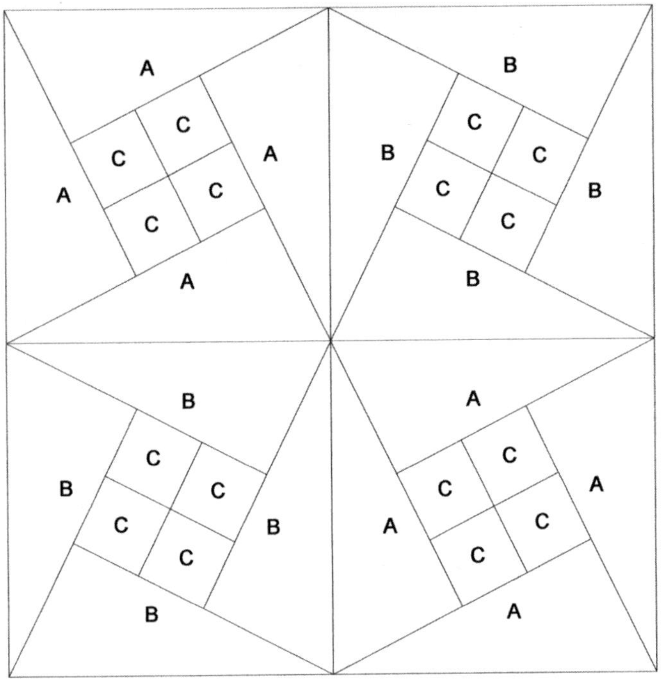

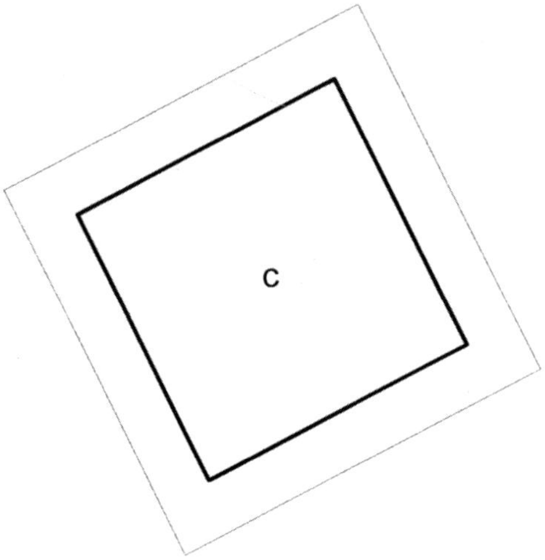

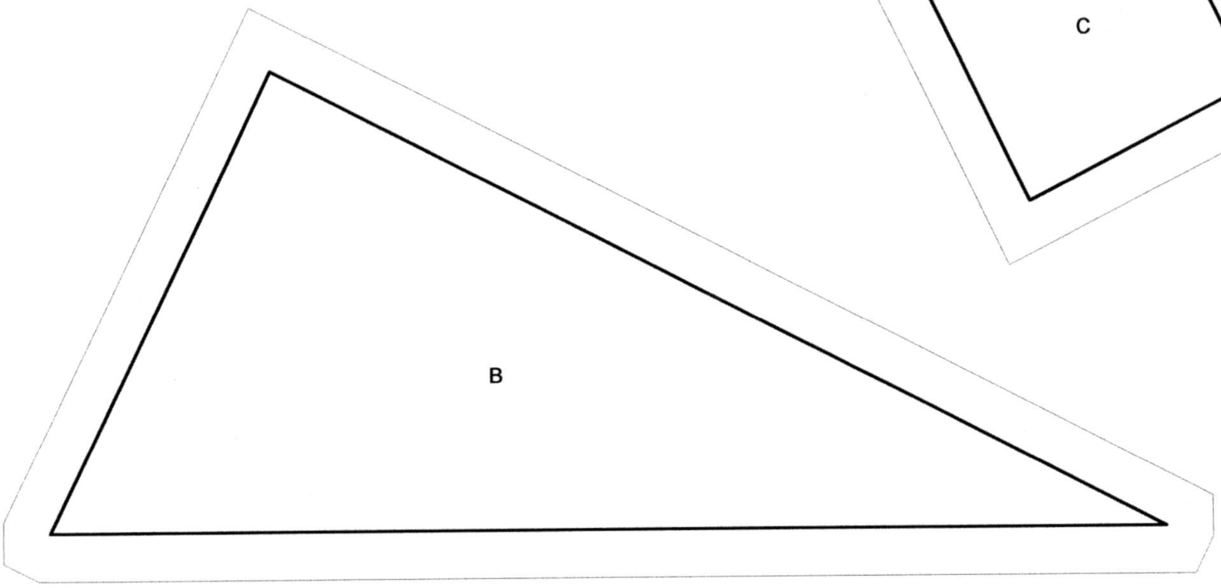

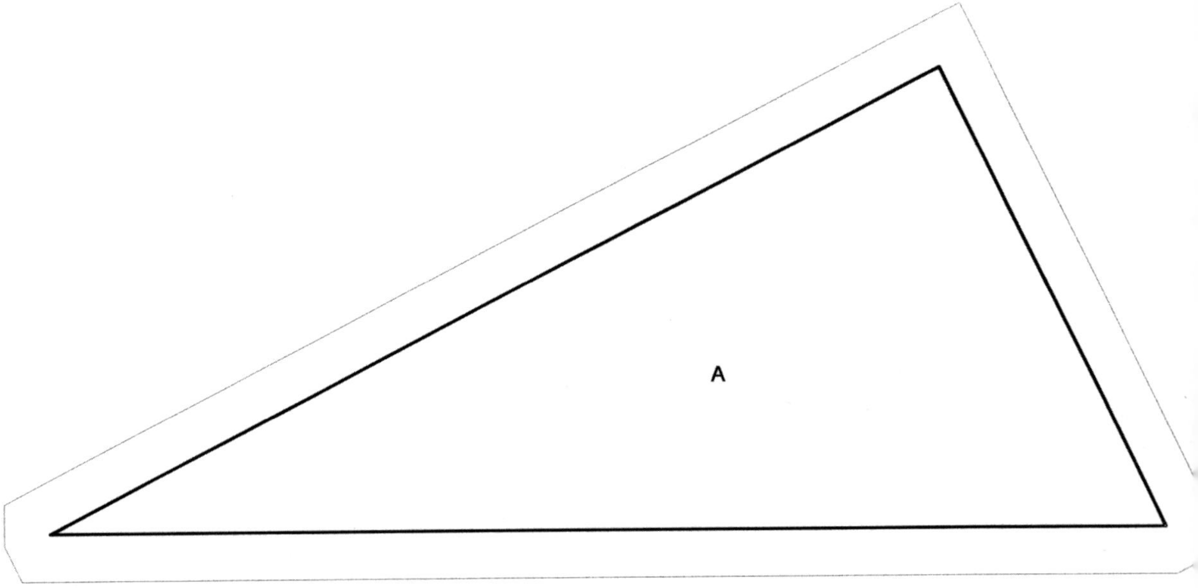

Arabic Lattice

Template

Appeared in The Star **May 22, 1935**

To Make the Block

1 Sew a dark A piece to either side of a light B piece. Make 4.

2 Sew the 4 quadrants together to complete the block.

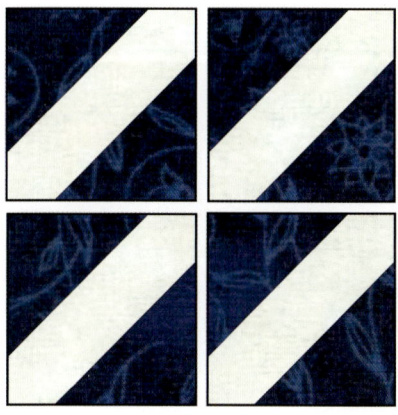

Indian Hatchet

Block Size: 12" finished

Fabric Needed

Dark

Light

For this pattern, we'll use templates because of the odd shape of piece B.

Cutting Instructions

From the dark fabric, cut

8 triangles using template A

From the light fabric, cut

4 pieces using template B

Indian Hatchet

From The Kansas City Star,

May 22, 1935:

No. 402

Original size – 6"

This is a quick pattern for summer work. All of the family can help with these straight strips. Good luck to you. Choose pretty colors. Every quilt is as artistic as the quiltmaker.

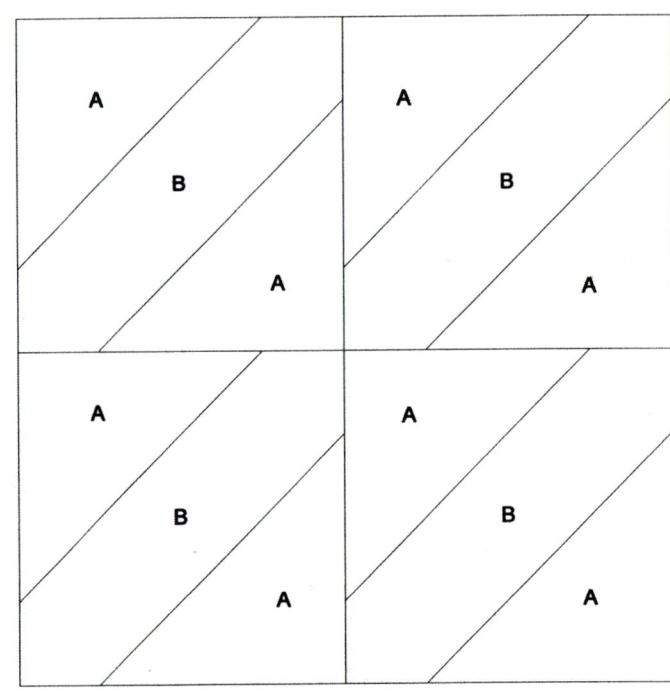

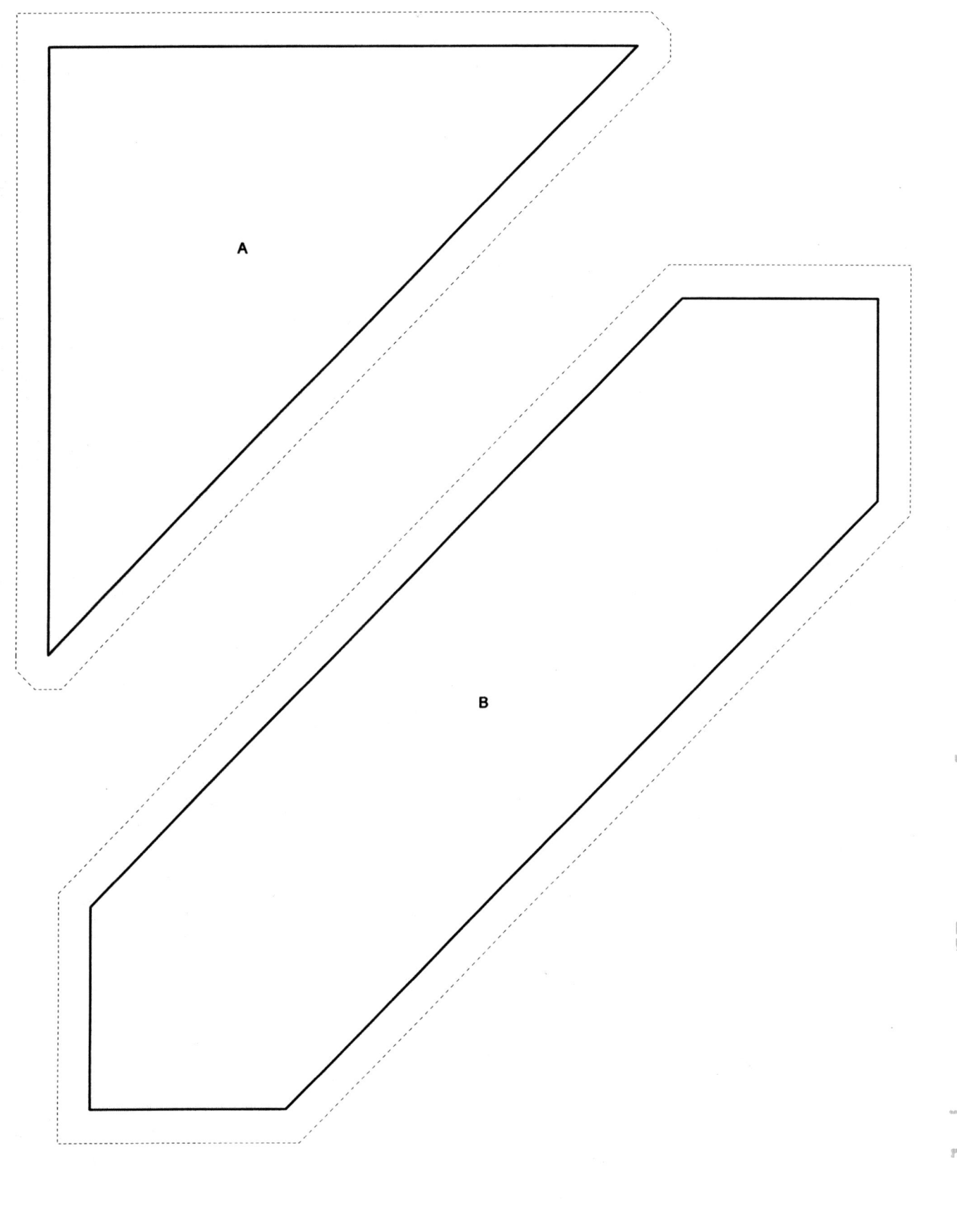

A

B

Indian Hatchet

Grandmother's Quilt

Grandmother's Quilt

Block Size: 12" finished

Fabric Needed

Black

Tan

Red

Cutting Instructions

From the tan fabric, cut

1 – 7 1/4" square. Cut the square from corner to corner twice on the diagonal or cut 4 triangles using template B

4 – 3 1/2" squares (template A)

18 – 1 1/2" squares (template D)

From the red fabric, cut

18 – 1 1/2" squares (template D)

From the black fabric, cut

4 – 3 7/8" squares. Cut each square from corner to corner once on the diagonal or cut 8 triangles using template C.

To Make the Block

1 Sew the 1 1/2" tan squares to the 1 1/2" red squares into rows of 6. Alternate the colors and make 6 rows.
This is the center of the block.

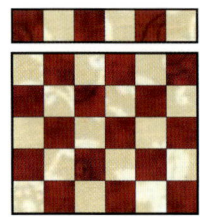

2 Sew a black C triangle to either side of a tan B triangle to make a flying geese unit. Make 4.

3 Sew a 3 1/2" A square to either side of a a flying geese unit. Make two rows like this.

4 Sew a flying geese unit to either side of the center checkerboard square to make the center row.

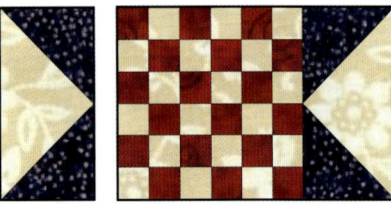

5 Sew the three rows together to complete the block.

From The Kansas City Star,

November 3, 1948:

No. 839

Original size – 12"

When Mrs. Claudie Gray, route 1, Qulin, Mo., married in 1903, one of her wedding gifts was a quilt in this pattern, pieced by her husband's mother during the latter part of the nineteenth centry, when the design was a general favorite.

History of the Block

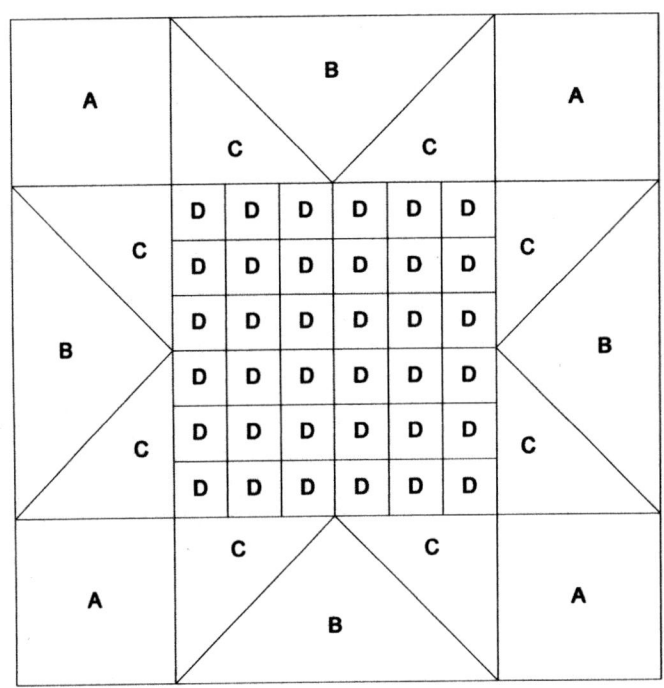

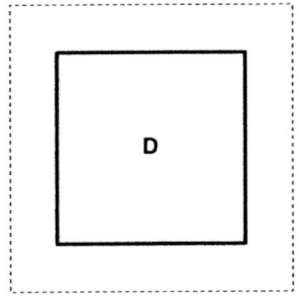

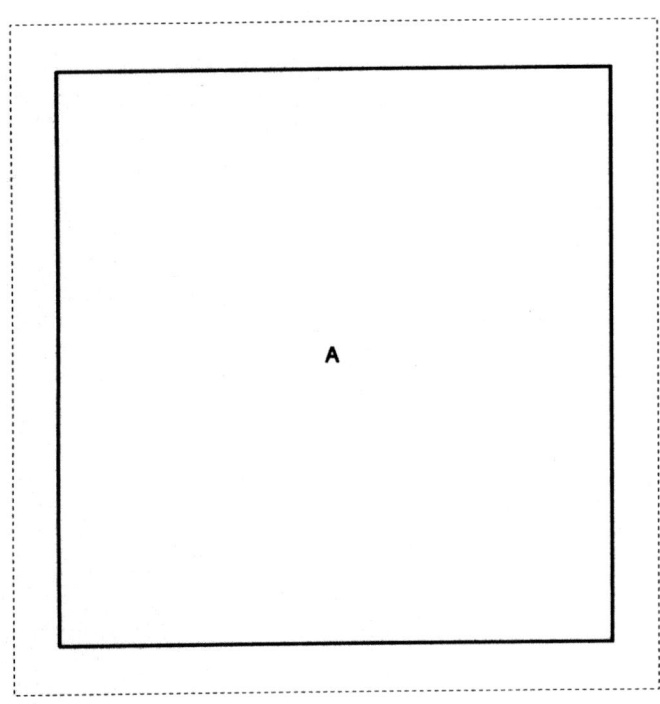

Template

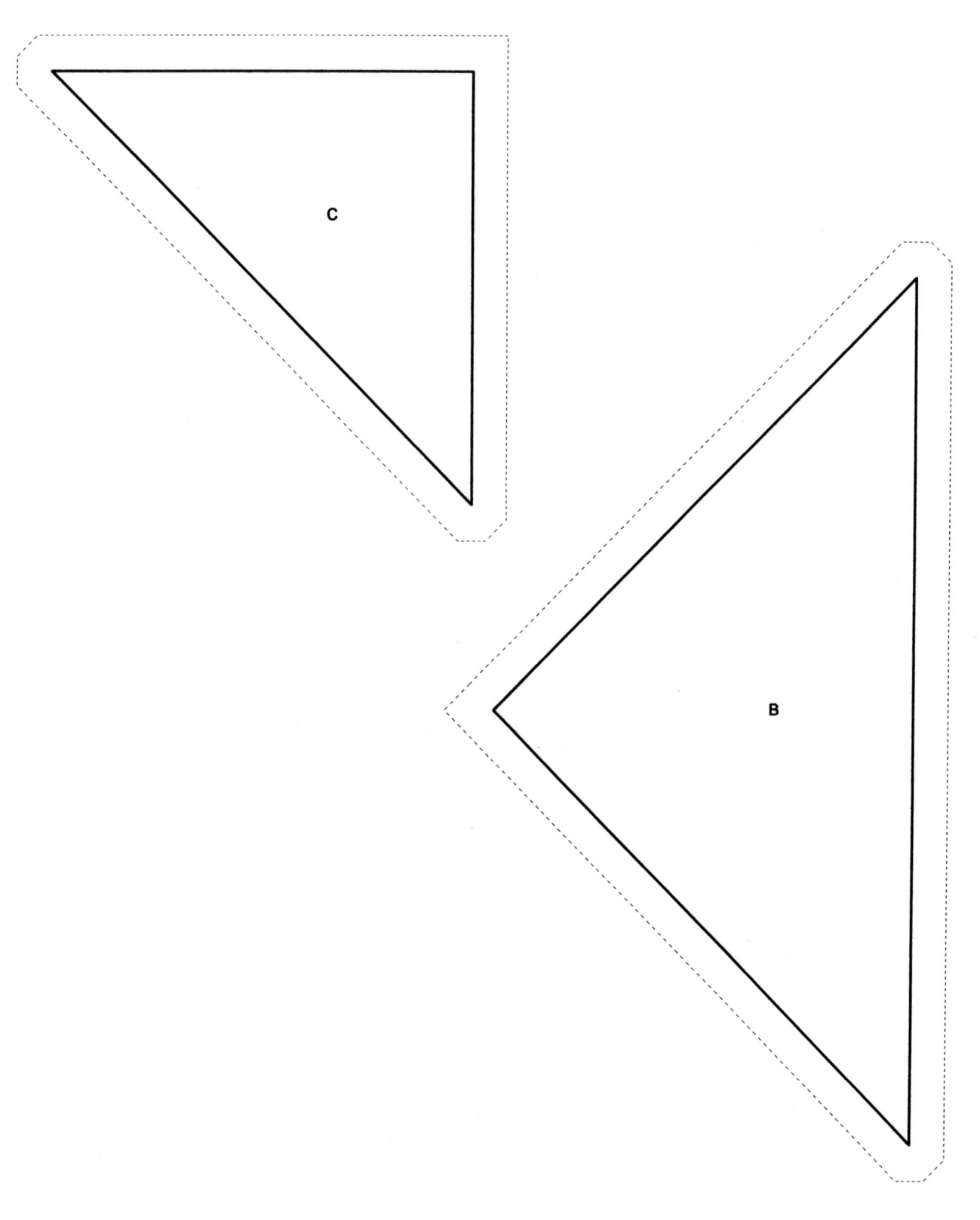

C

B

Grandmother's Quilt

Appeared in The Star **June 14, 1939**

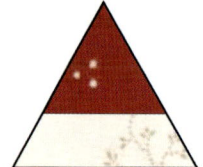

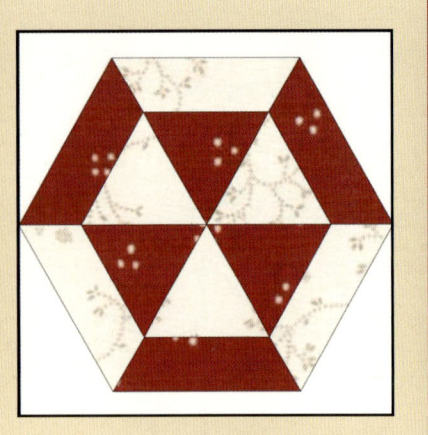

Hexagon Beauty

Block Size: 12" finished

Fabric Needed

Red

Cream

Note: The finished measurement is obtained by measuring from point to point.

We'll make this block using templates.

Cutting Instructions

From the red fabric, cut

3 pieces using template A

3 pieces using template B

From the cream fabric, cut

3 pieces using template A

3 pieces using template B

To Make the Block

1

Sew a red A piece to a cream B piece. Make 3.

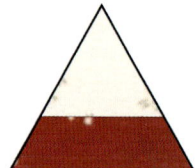

2

Sew a cream A piece to a red B piece. Make 3.

3

Sew three wedges together, alternating the colors. Make 2.

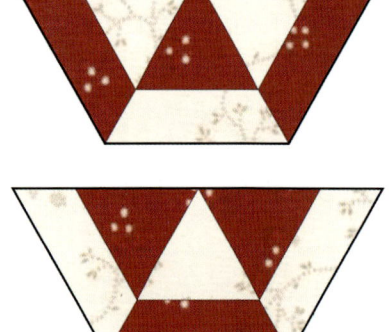

Hexagon Beauty

4 Sew the two sections together to complete the block.

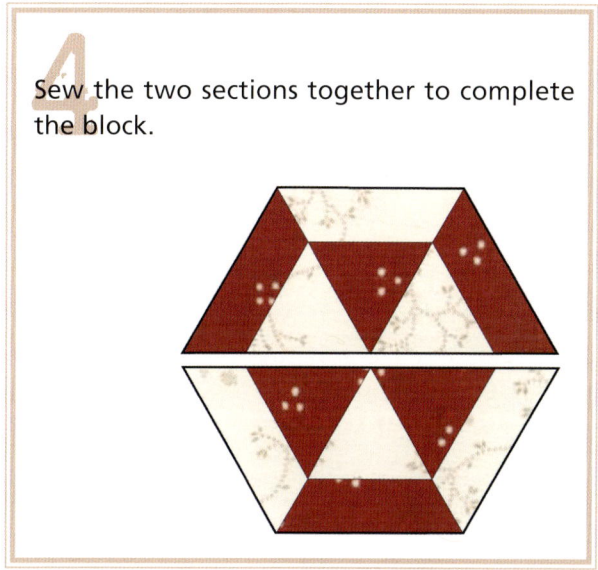

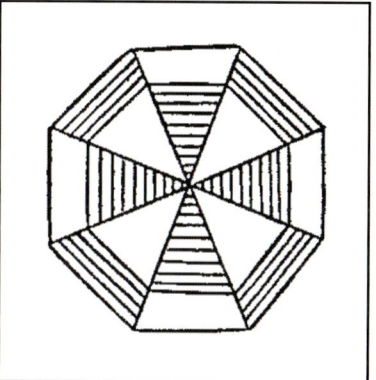

From The Kansas City Star, June 14, 1939:

No. 581

Original size – 10"

This pattern is contributed by Miss Alta M. House, Manchester, Kas.

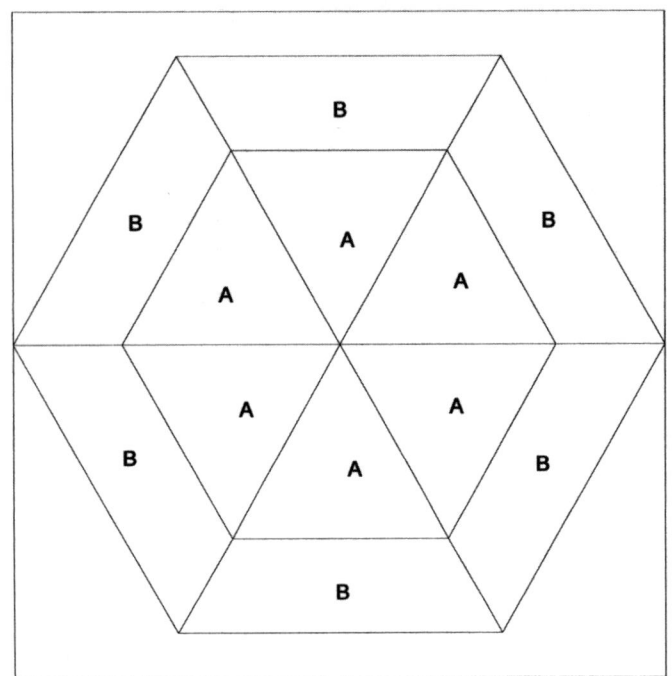

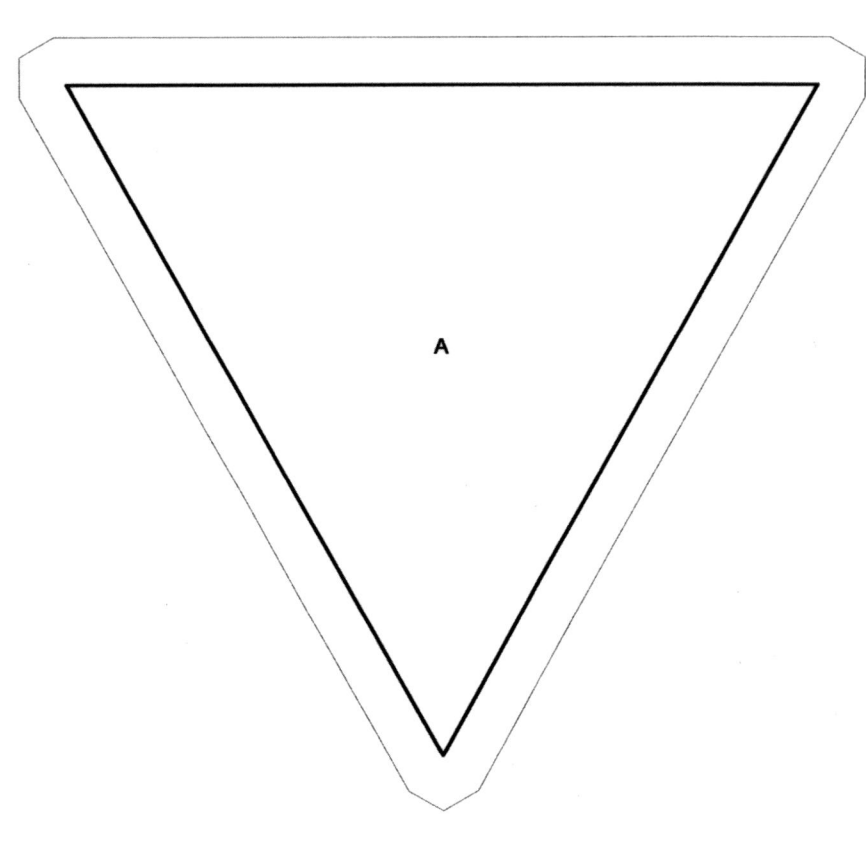

A

Template

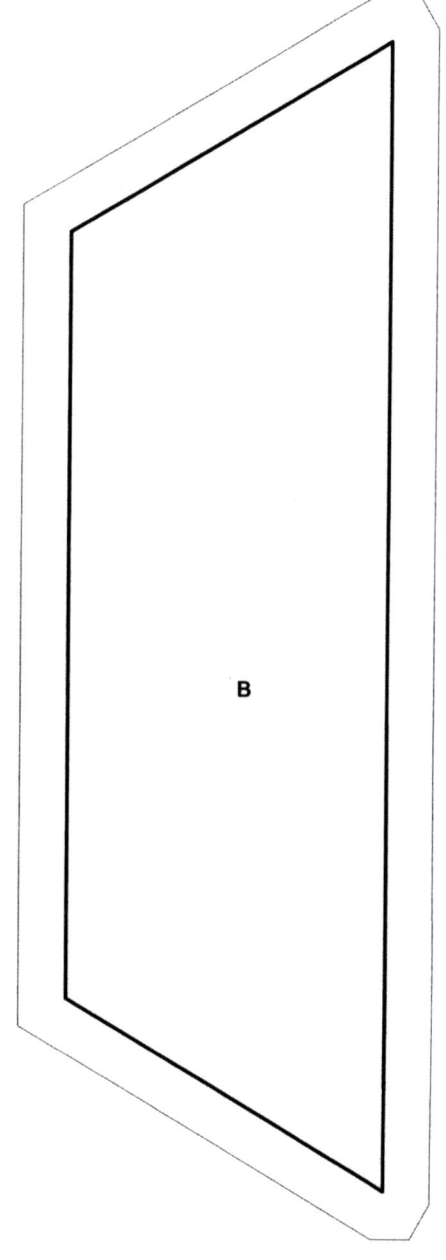

B

Template

Appeared in The Star **July 17, 1937**

Indian Star

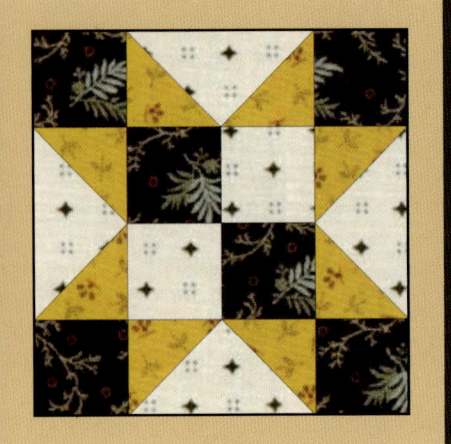

Indian Star

Block Size: 6" finished

Fabric Needed

Gold

Black

Shirting

Cutting Instructions

From the black fabric, cut

6 – 2" squares (template A)

From the gold fabric, cut

4 – 2 3/8" squares. Cut each square from corner to corner once on the diagonal or use template C.

From the shirting fabric, cut

2 – 2" squares (template A)

1 – 4 1/4" square. Cut the square from corner to corner twice on the diagonal or cut 4 triangles using template B.

To Make the Block

1 Sew 2 gold C triangles to a B triangle as shown below to make a flying geese unit. Make 4.

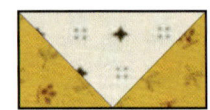

2 Make the center of the block by sewing a shirting square to a black square. Make 2 and sew them together as shown to make a 4-patch.

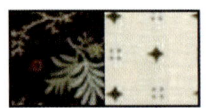

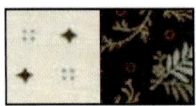

3 Sew a black square to either side of a flying geese unit. Make 2 strips like this.

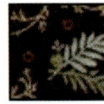

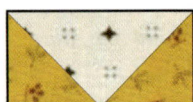

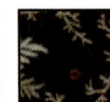

4 Sew a flying geese unit to either side of the 4-patch unit. Make 1 strip.

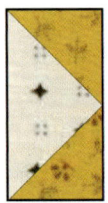

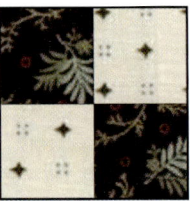

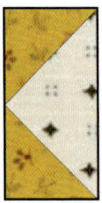

5 Sew the three strips together to complete the block.

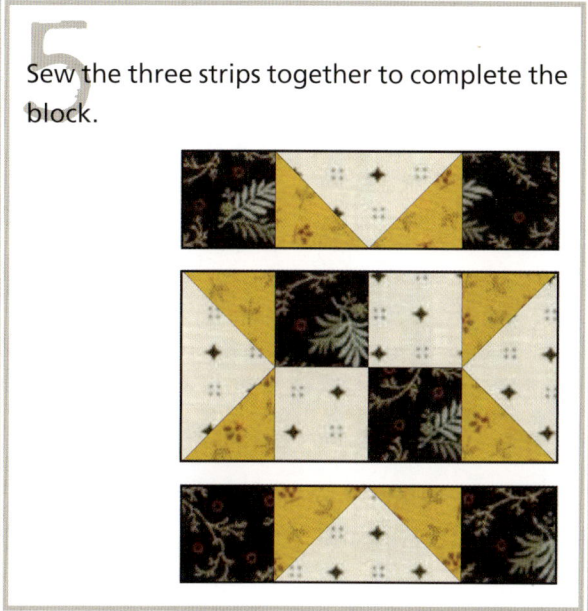

From The Kansas City Star,

July 17, 1937:

No. 511

Original size – 6"

Here is another version of the ever popular star design for a quilt. This pattern was contributed by Miss Genevieve Taylor, Bolivar, Mo.

History of the Block

"Indian Star" stitched by Jane Miller, Lee's Summit, Mo. and quilted by Chuck McDowell, Blue Springs, Mo. Pattern from book "Nickel Quilts: Great Designs from 5-inch Scraps" by Pat Speth and Charlene Thode, Martingale & Company, published 2002.

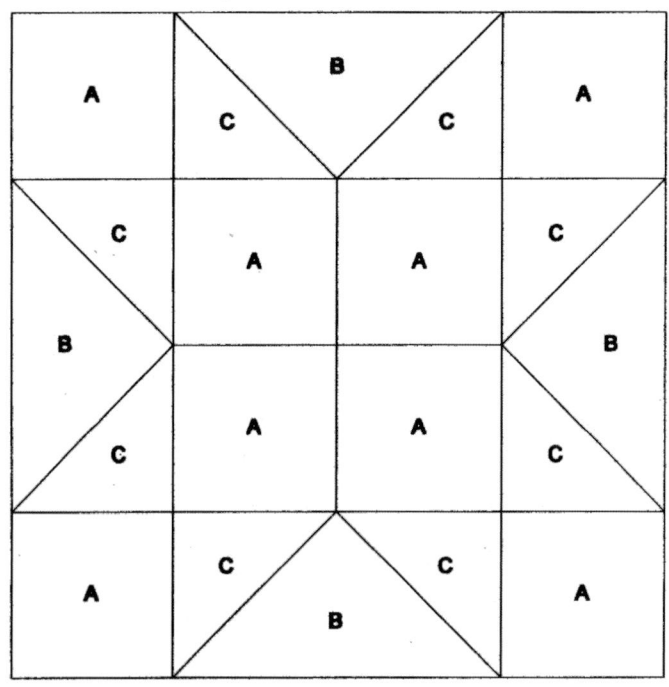

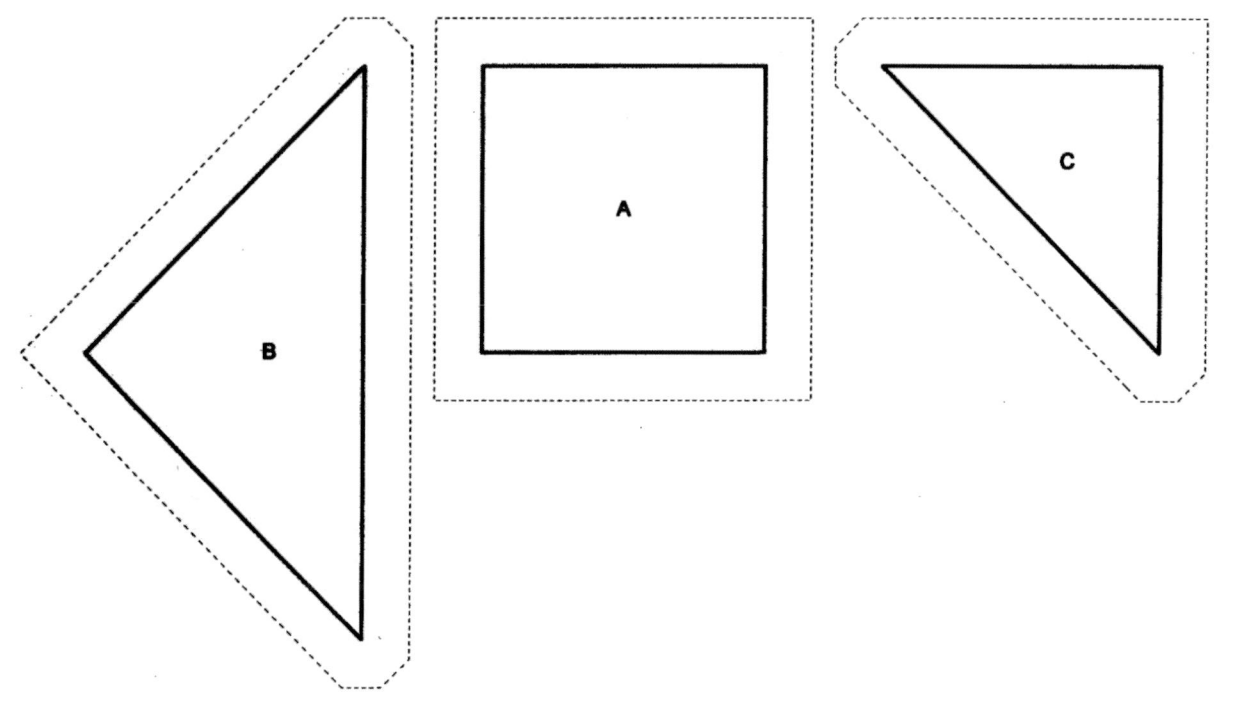

Indian Star

Template

Appeared in The Star **September 14, 1955**

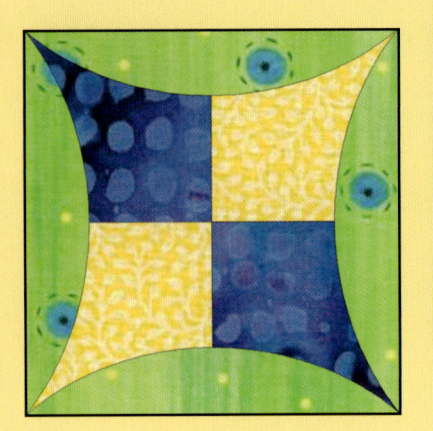

Moon is New

Block Size: 6" finished

Fabric Needed

Blue

Yellow

Green

For this pattern, we'll use templates because of the odd shapes.

Cutting Instructions

From the blue fabric, cut

2 pieces using template B

From the yellow fabric, cut

2 pieces using template B

From the green fabric, cut

4 pieces using template A

To Make the Block

1

Sew a blue B piece to a yellow B piece as shown. Make 2.

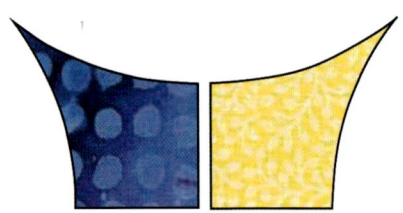

2

Sew the 2 units together and add the green A pieces to complete the block.

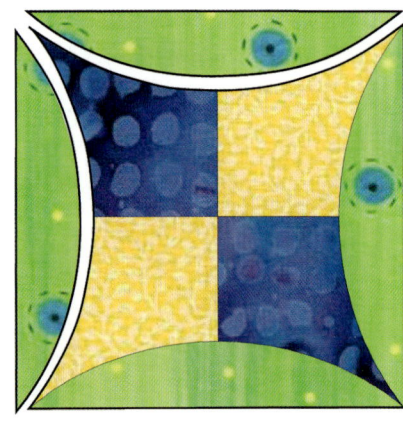

Moon is New

From The Kansas City Star,

September 14, 1955:

No. 961

Original size – 11 1/2"

Mrs. W. A. Middleton, route 2, Checotah, Ok., sets her New Moon blocks together with 3-inch strips of fabric. Blue would be an appropriate color for the 1-tone pieces and a small print in which yellow predominates could be a harmonious choice for the New Moon pieces.

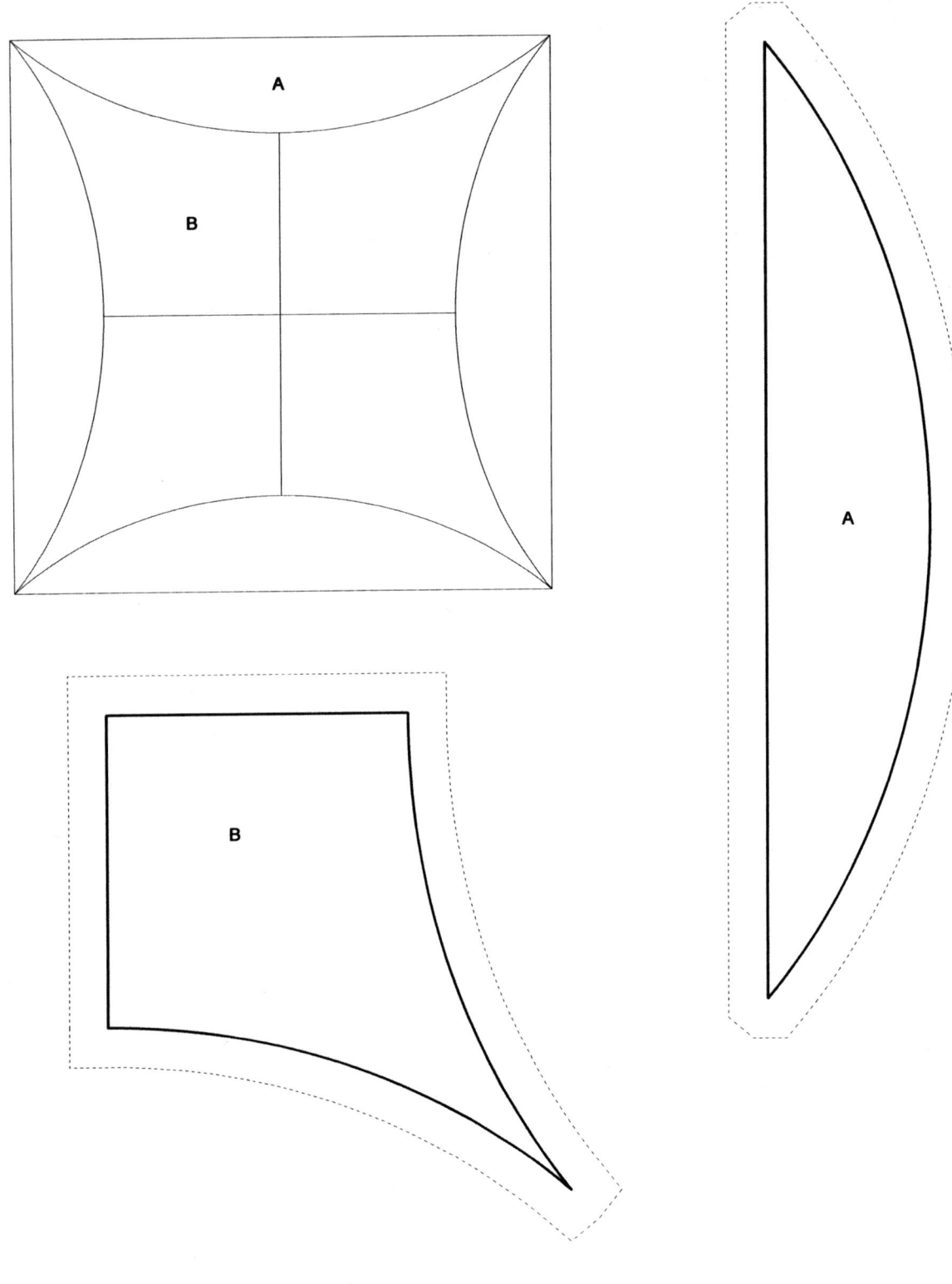

A

B

B

A

Template

Appeared in The Star **May 8, 1940**

Comfort Quilt

Block Size: 9" finished

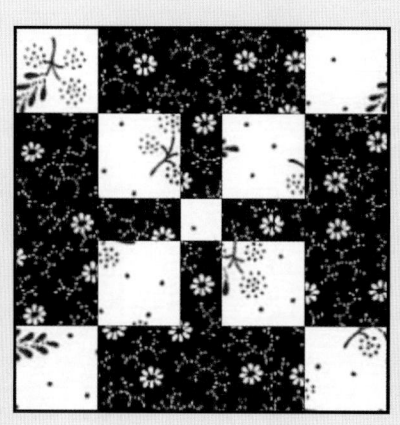

Fabric Needed

Navy blue print

Blue and white shirting

To Make the Block

1 Begin with the center of the block. Sew a 2 1/2" A square to either side of a navy blue C rectangle. Make 2.

 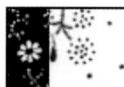

2 Sew a navy blue rectangle to either side of the 1 1/2" D shirting square.

3 Sew the three rows together.

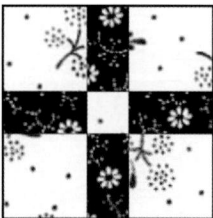

4 Sew a navy blue B rectangle to either side of the center of the block as shown.

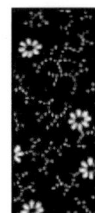 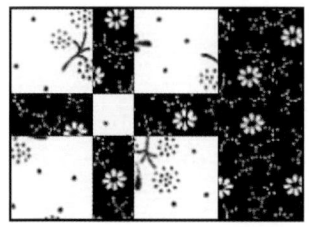

Cutting Instructions

From the shirting fabric, cut

8 - 2 1/2" squares or use template A

1 – 1 1/2" square or use template D

From the navy blue fabric, cut

4 - 2 1/2" x 5 1/2" rectangles or use template B

4 – 1 1/2" x 2 1/2" rectangles or use template C

Comfort Quilt

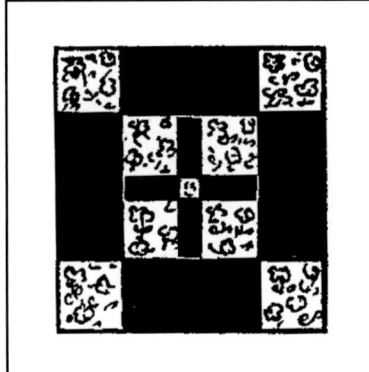

From The Kansas City Star,

May 8, 1940:

No. 614

Original Size - 11".

Because this design is adapted to either a quilt or comfort top, Mrs. David M. Lintner, Warwick, Ia., has named it "The Comfort Quilt." One of her comfort tops in this pattern is made with the 1-tone pieces in rich purple, the other a print in which purple and gold are the predominating colors.

5

Sew a 2 1/2" A square to either end of a navy blue B rectangle. Make 2. Sew one to the top of the block and one to the bottom.

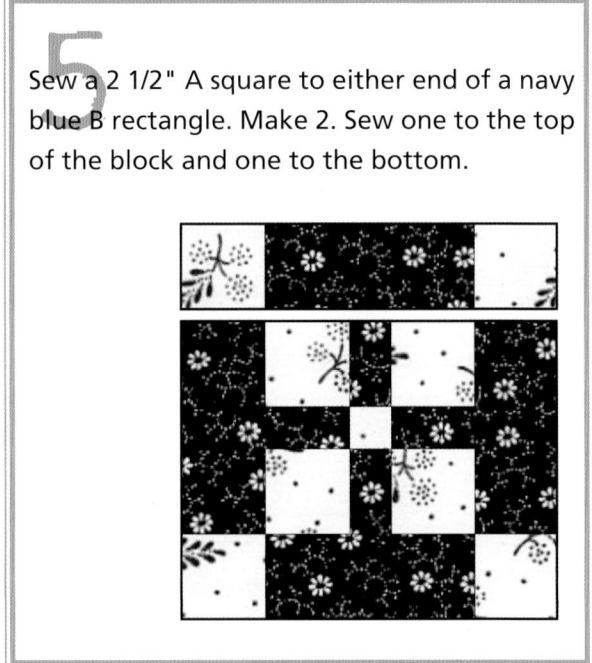

Template

Grandmother's Cross

Block Size: 12" finished

Fabric Needed

Cream

Tan

Medium brown

Dark brown

Grandmother's Cross *(vertical title, left margin)*

Cutting Instructions

From the cream fabric, cut

10 – 2 5/8" squares (template C)

From the tan fabric, cut

2 – 3 7/8" squares. Cut each square once from corner to corner once on the diagonal or cut 4 triangles using template A.

2 – 2 5/8" squares (template C)

From the medium brown fabric, cut

1 - 7 1/4" square. Cut the square twice from corner to corner on the diagonal or cut 4 triangles using template B.

From the dark brown fabric, cut

8 – 2 5/8" squares (template C)

To Make the Block

1 Sew the cream and dark brown 2 5/8" squares together into 4-patch units as shown. Make four.

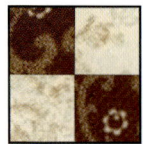

2 Sew the cream and tan 2 5/8" squares together into a 4-patch unit as shown. Make one.

3 We'll sew the block together on the diagonal. Sew a medium brown B triangle to either side of a 4-patch as shown. Make two rows like this.

4 Sew three 4-patch units together as shown.

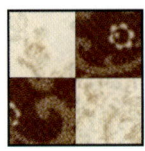  

5 Sew the three rows together.

6 Add a tan A triangle to each corner to complete the block.

From The Kansas City Star,

June 20, 1947:

No. 767

Original size – 8 1/4"

The colors of the triangular pieces in Grandmother's Cross may be in reverse of those suggested; those at the tip of each bar being dark, and the larger ones between bars, light. Contributor of the design is Mrs. Ellen Hargraves, Warren, Ark.

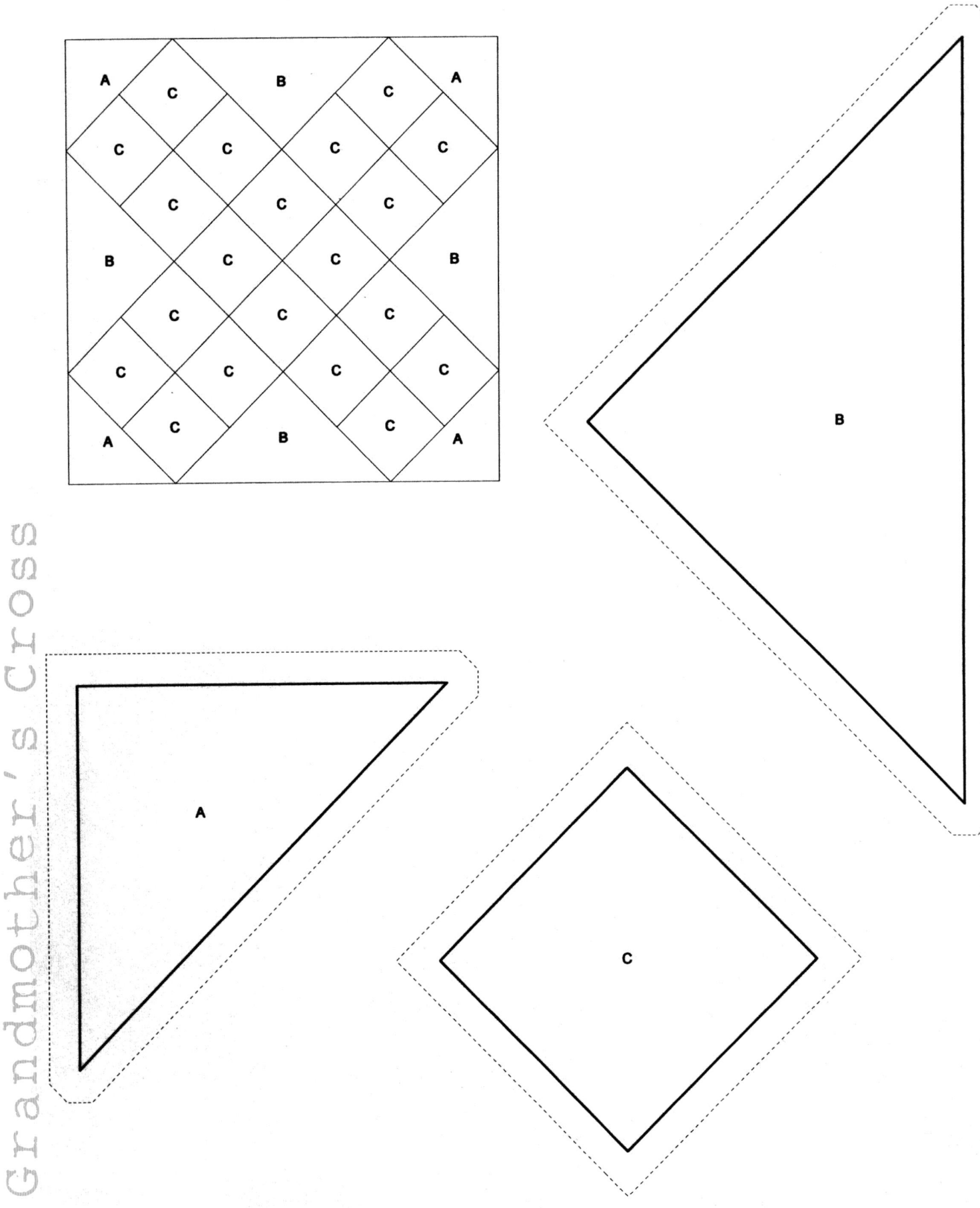

Grandmother's Cross

Template

Appeared in The Star **September 14, 1955**

Rose Cross

Block Size: 15" finished

Fabric Needed

Background fabric

Pink

Rose

Green

Yellow

To Make the Block

1 Fold the background fabric in quarters from corner to corner on the diagonal and press the creases in lightly for placement purposes.

Prepare the appliqué pieces using the appliqué method of your choice.

Pin the appliqué elements in place and stitch.

When you are done with the appliqué work, press the block and trim to 15 1/2".

Cutting Instructions – add 1/8" – 1/4" seam allowances to all pieces

From the pink, cut

4 buds

1 flower

From the green, cut

16 leaves

4 calyx

4 – 1/2" x 4" bias strips for the stems

From the rose, cut

1 outer flower

1 – 16 1/2" background square

From yellow, cut

1 flower center

Rose Cross

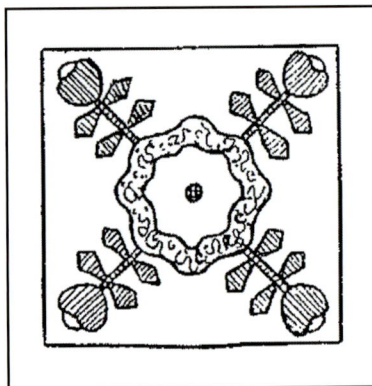

From The Kansas City Star,

September 14, 1955:

No. 80

Original Size - 15"
Applique quilting is one of the most popular branches of the art and it is for lovers of applique that the "Rose Crown" is offered. Unlike piecing, applique offers diversifications and embellishments. The patterns may be made just as elaborate as the maker chooses and her originality has more chance to assert itself. This pattern shows a decorative combination of a cross motif and a foundation rose pattern. The colors are optional but there is no prettier combination than the ones suggested here in yellow, rose and pink with the leaves developed in green. Of all the patterns developed from the rose as a central foundation this is one of the most charming.

PINK

GREEN

ROSE

PINK

YELLOW

GREEN

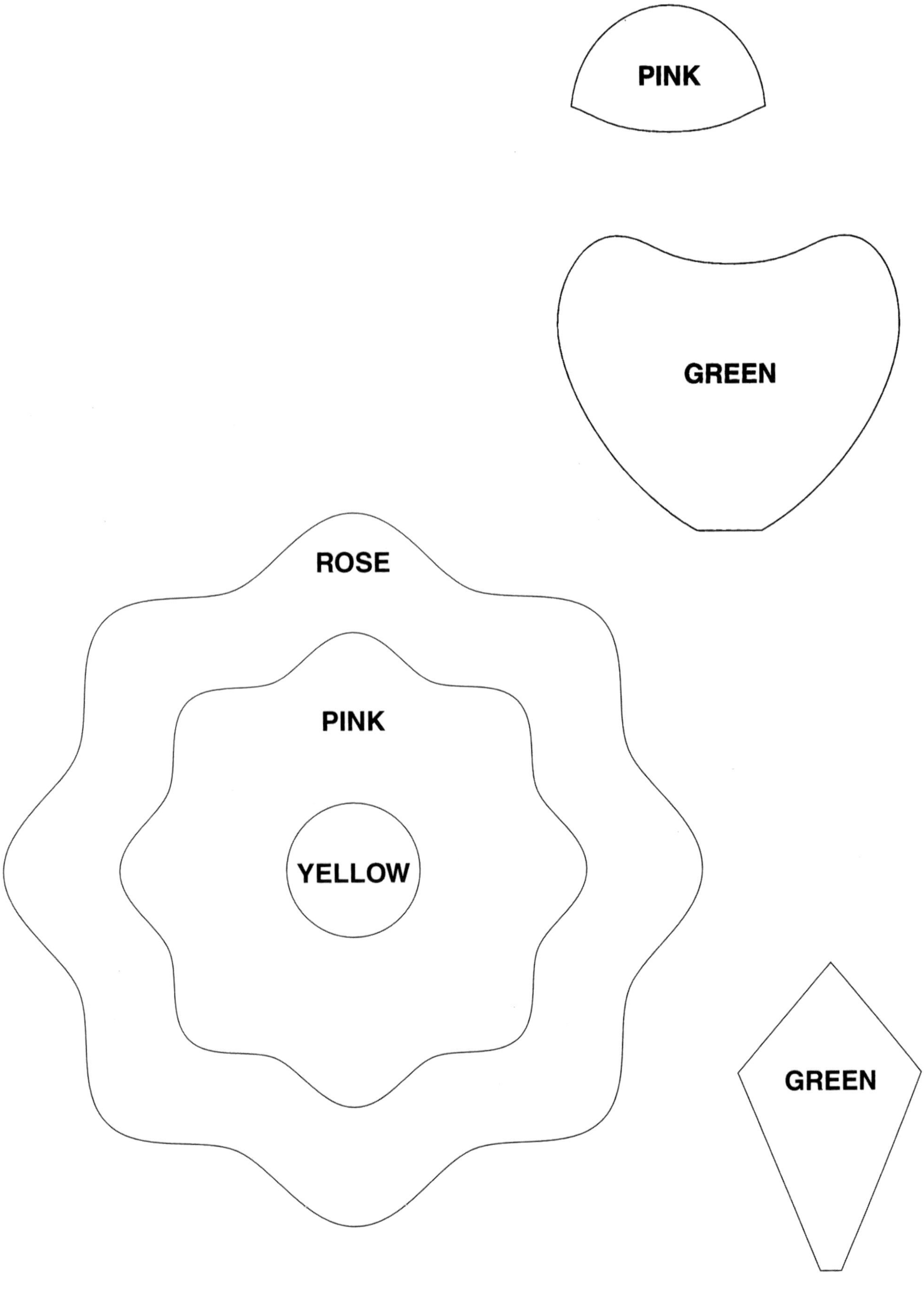

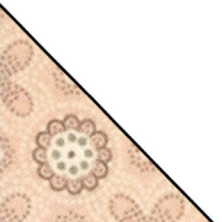

Signature Quilt

Block Size: 6" finished

Fabric Needed

Brown

Pink

Light tan

We'll make this block using templates because of the oddly shaped piece that goes in the middle of the block.

Cutting Instructions

From the brown fabric, cut

2 triangles using template A

From the pink fabric, cut

2 triangles using template A

From the light tan fabric, cut

1 piece using template B

To Make the Block

1

Sew a pink A piece to a brown A piece. Make 2.

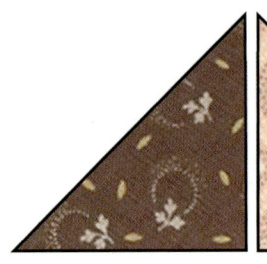

2

Sew a pink/brown unit to either side of the light tan B strip to complete the block.

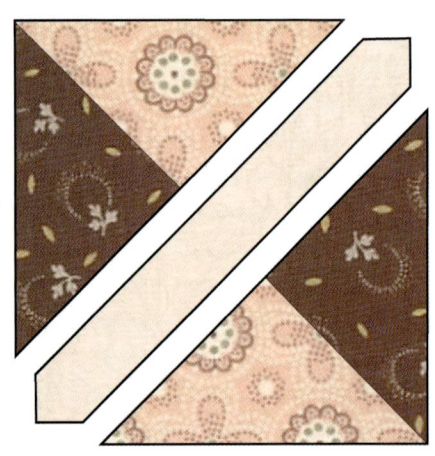

Signature Quilt

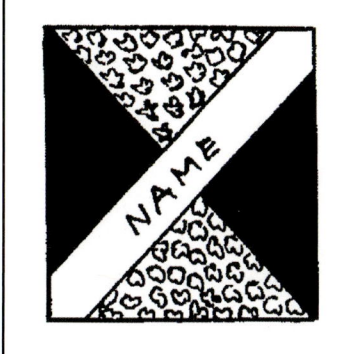

From The Kansas City Star,

February 10, 1954:

No. 935

Original size – 7 1/2"
Everything to be desired for a friendship signature quilt is included in this pattern. There is a long white strip for the name, there are print blocks and 1-tone pieces, with the choice of color left to the needlecrafter. The block was designed by Mrs. Clyde Offutt, Sleeper, Mo., for her daughter, Miss Dixie L. Offutt.

A

A

B

A

A

B

A

Appeared in The Star **August 27, 1952**

To Make the Block

Make a template for each apron piece. Add 1/4" seam allowance on all sides.

Cut out each apron piece. Sew the pieces together. Align the top edge of the apron with the top edge of the background fabric and appliqué the sides and bottom of the apron to the background.

Note: For a 3-dimensional look, you can hem the bottom edge of the apron rather appliquéing it down.

Sew the green strip to the top of the apron to complete the block.

My Mother's Apron

Block Size: 8" finished

Fabric Needed

Cream

Green

6 Scraps of your choice

This is an appliqué block.

Cutting Directions

From the cream fabric, cut

1 – 7 1/2" x 8 1/2" rectangle

From the green fabric, cut

1 – 1 1/2" x 8 1/2" rectangle

From the scraps, cut

1 apron piece per color

My Mother's Apron

From The Kansas City Star,

August 27, 1952:

No. 912

Original Size - 6 3/4" x 7 3/8"

No one should object being tied to the strings of an apron as pretty as this one designed by Mrs. Ted Capps, Sallisaw, Ok.

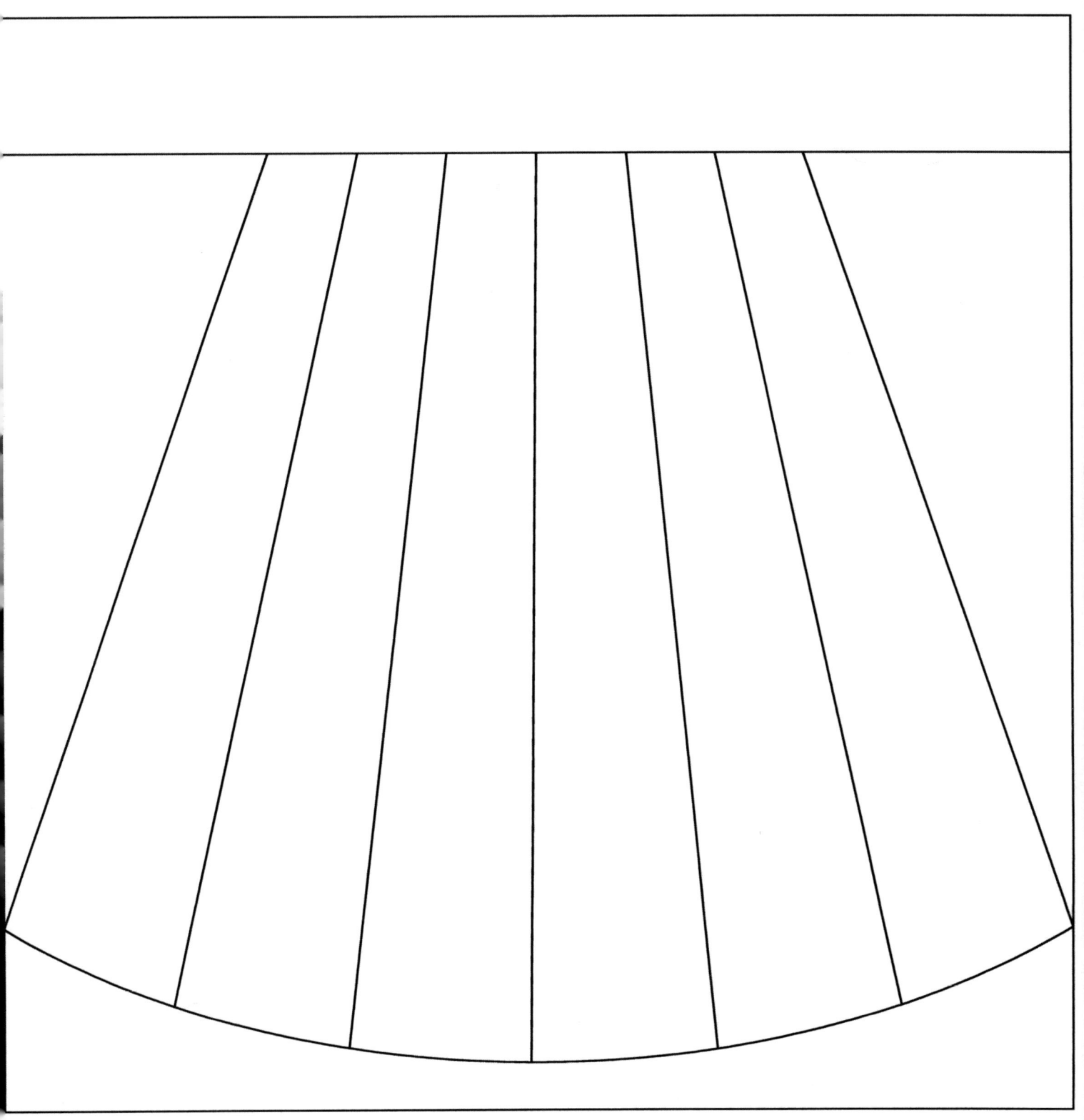

My Mother's Apron

Template

Rose Bud

Block Size: 12" finished

Fabric Needed

Light pink

Dark pink

Green

Cream

You'll be able to make this block using rotary cutting directions.

Cutting Instructions

From the light pink fabric, cut

4 – 2" squares (template A)

From the dark pink fabric, cut

12 – 2" squares (template A)

From the green fabric, cut

8 – 2" squares (template A)

From the cream fabric, cut

4 – 2" x 6 1/2" rectangles (template B)

4 – 2" x 3 1/2" rectangles (template C)

1 – 6 1/2" square

To Make the Block

1 Sew 1 light pink 2" square to 3 dark pink 2" squares as shown to make a 4-patch unit. Make 4.

2 Sew a green 2" square to either end of a cream C rectangle as shown. Make 4.

3 Sew a cream B rectangle onto each of the green and cream units.

4 Add a 4-patch unit to either end of two of the rectangle units as shown.

Rose Bud

5 Sew a rectangle unit to either side of the center square.

6 Sew the three rows together to complete the block.

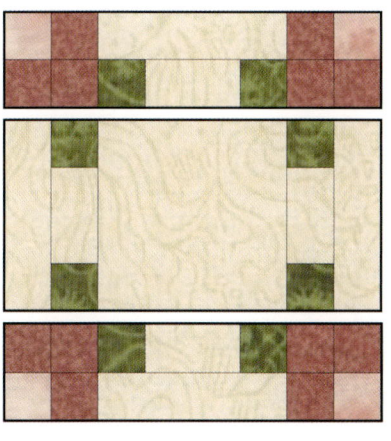

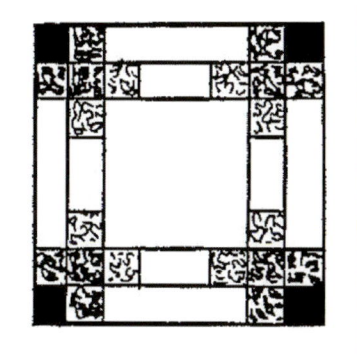

From The Kansas City Star,

May 3, 1942:

No. 686

Original size – 12"

This blocked conception of a rosebud is the offering of Eunice P. Turner, Fowler, Kas. White may be used for the 1-tone blocks, but a harmonizing contrast in another color could also be supplied with pleasing effect.

History of the Block

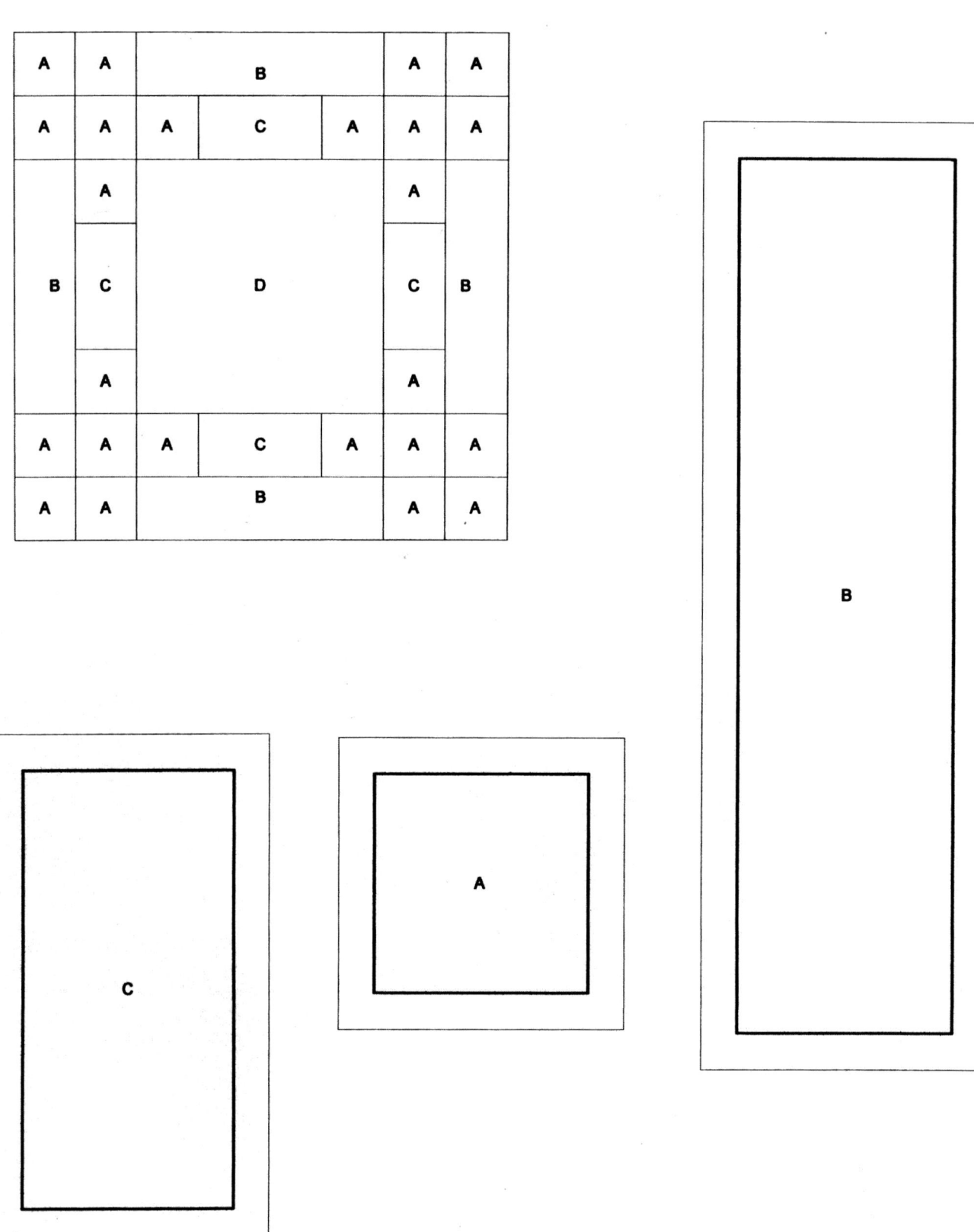

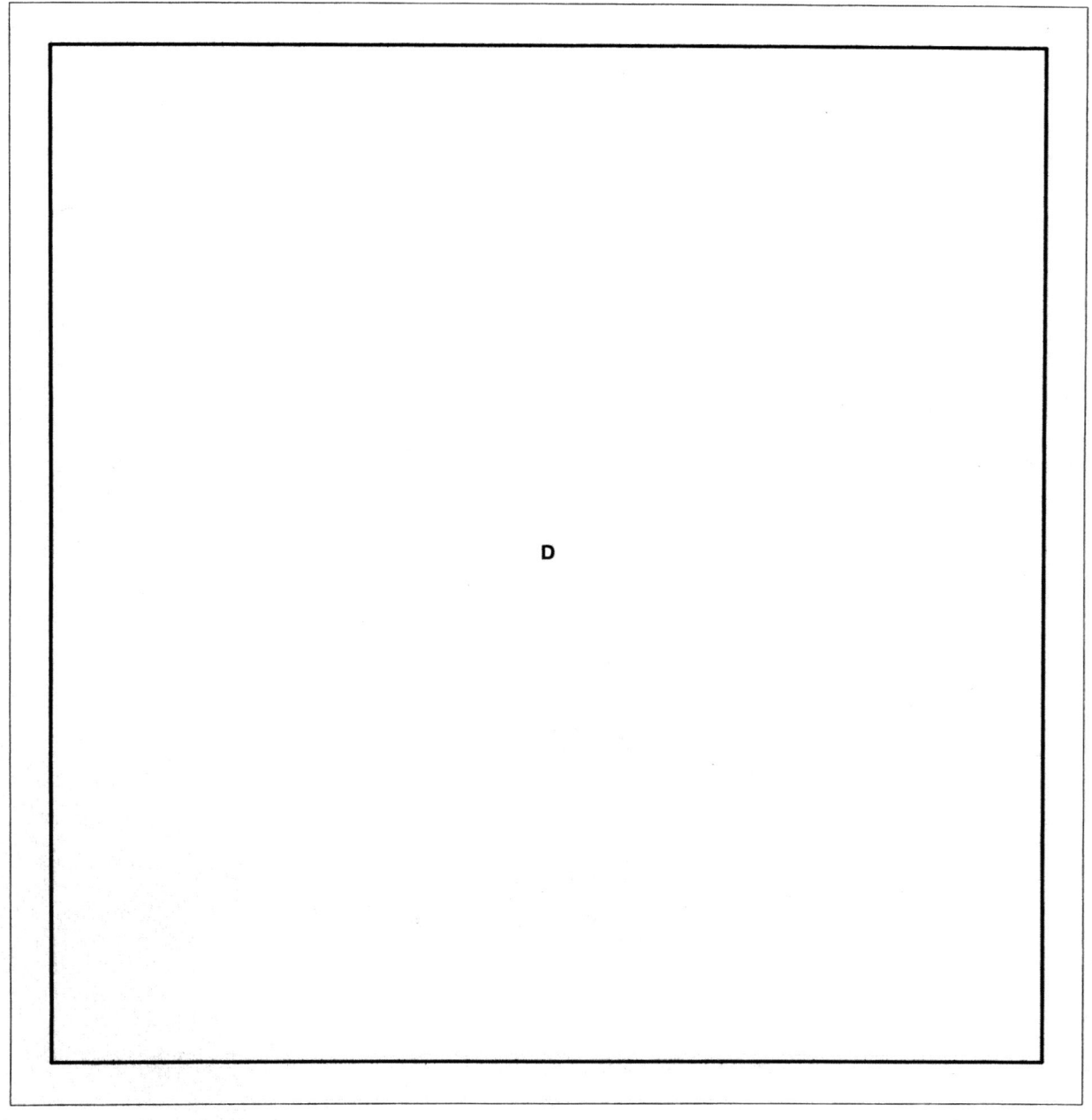

D

Appeared in The Star **April 17, 1935**

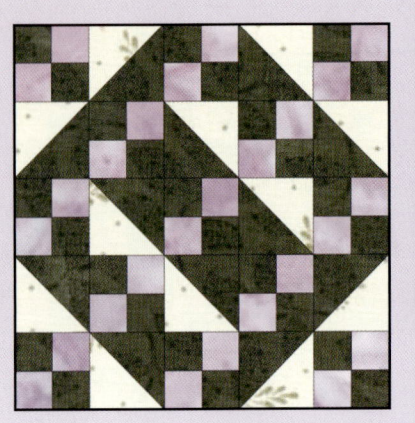

Ozark Trail

Block Size: 15" finished

Fabric Needed

Dark green

Lavender

Green/cream shirting

This block can be made using rotary cutting directions.

Cutting Instructions

From the dark green fabric, cut

26 – 2″ squares (template A)

6 – 3 7/8″ squares or 12 triangles using template B

From the green/cream shirting fabric, cut

6 – 3 7/8″ squares or 12 triangles using template B

From the lavender fabric, cut

26 – 2″ squares (template A)

Ozark Trail

To Make the Block

1

You will need to make 12 shirting/dark green half-square triangle units. To make the half-square triangles, draw a line from corner to corner on the reverse side of the shirting 3 7/8″ triangles. Place a shirting square atop a dark green square and sew 1/4″ on either side of the drawn line. Using a rotary cutter, cut along the drawn line. Open each unit and press toward the darker fabric. If you cut your triangles separately, sew a shirting B triangle to a dark green B triangle. Make 12 units.

2

Sew the green 2″ A squares to the lavender A squares to make 4-patch units. Make 13.

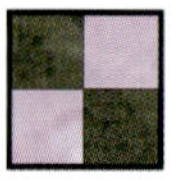

3

Sew the 4-patch units and the half-square triangle units into rows as shown below.

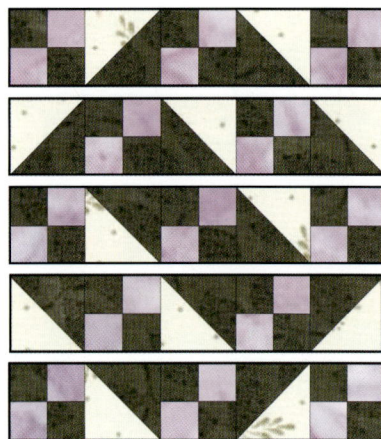

Sew the five rows together to complete the block.

From The Kansas City Star,

April 17, 1935 :

No. 397

Original size – 16"

As many lovers of out-of-doors follow the Ozark trail in spring and autumn, a quilt fan has given this name to a 16-inch block. Mrs. Marjorie Berry, Galt, Mo., sends this pattern.

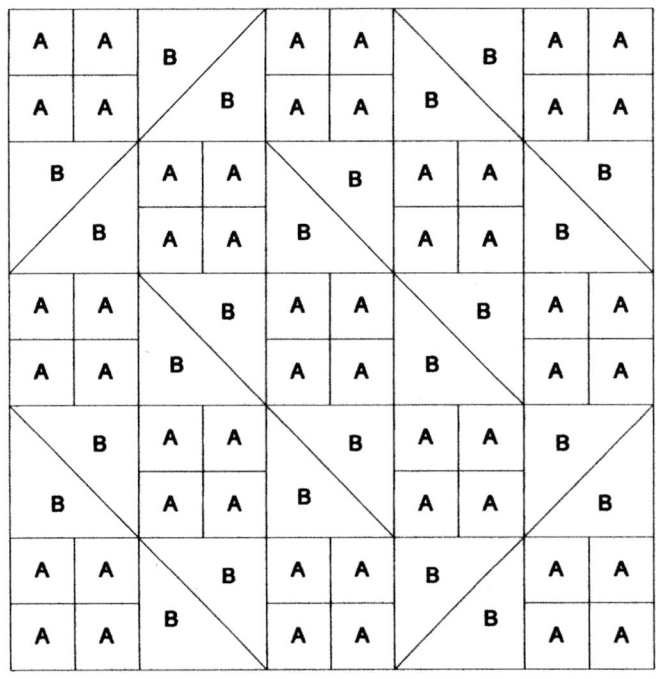

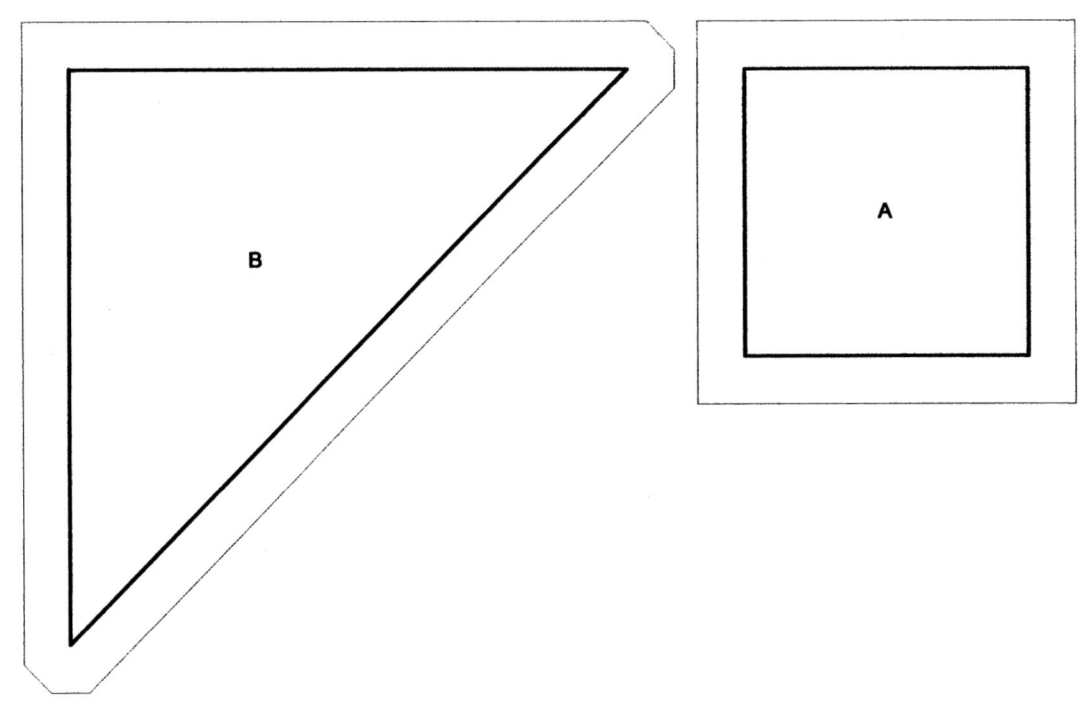

Template

Appeared in The Star **July 9, 1941**

Periwinkle

Block Size: 9" finished

Fabric Needed

Medium blue

Light blue

Cream

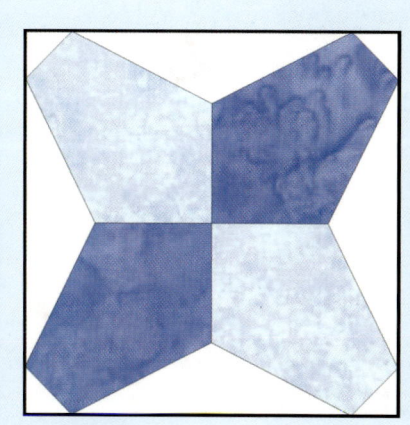

You'll need templates for this block.

Cutting Directions

From the cream fabric, cut

4 pieces using template A

4 pieces using template B

From the medium blue fabric, cut

2 pieces using template C

From the light blue fabric, cut

2 pieces using template C

To Make the Block

1

Sew the light blue and medium blue C pieces together as shown.

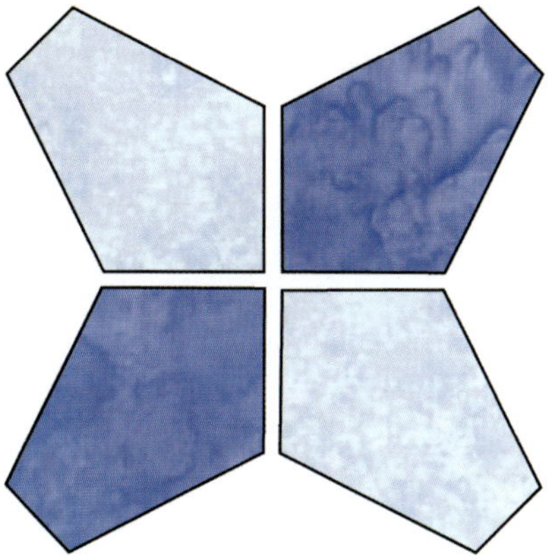

2

Inset the cream-colored B triangles.

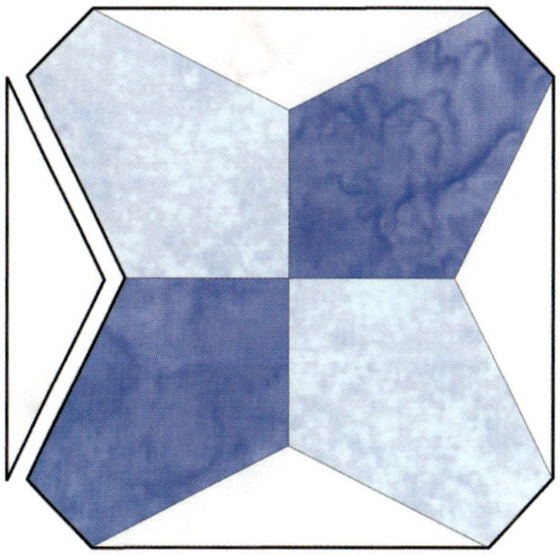

Periwinkle

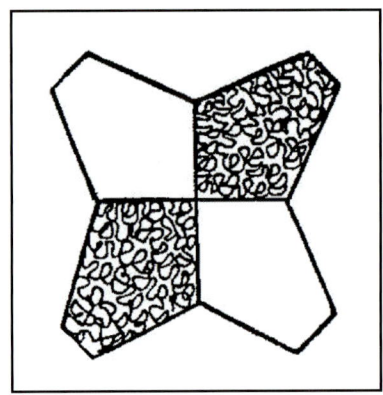

History of the Block

From The Kansas City Star,

July 9, 1941:

No. 652

Original Size - 5 5/8"
After the blocks are pieced, they
are joined with the hexagon. Mrs.
G. S. Ray, R. R. No. 2, Hollis,
Ok., who originated this design,
says either white or a 1-tone piece
can be used for the hexagon.

3
Sew a cream A triangle to each corner to
complete the block.

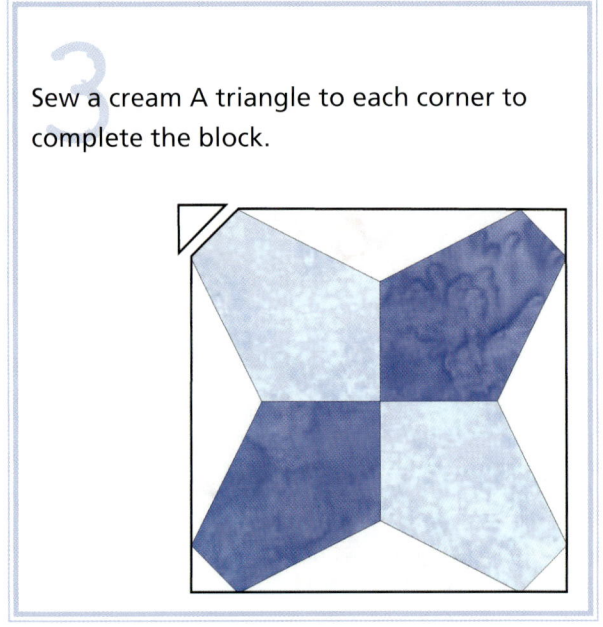

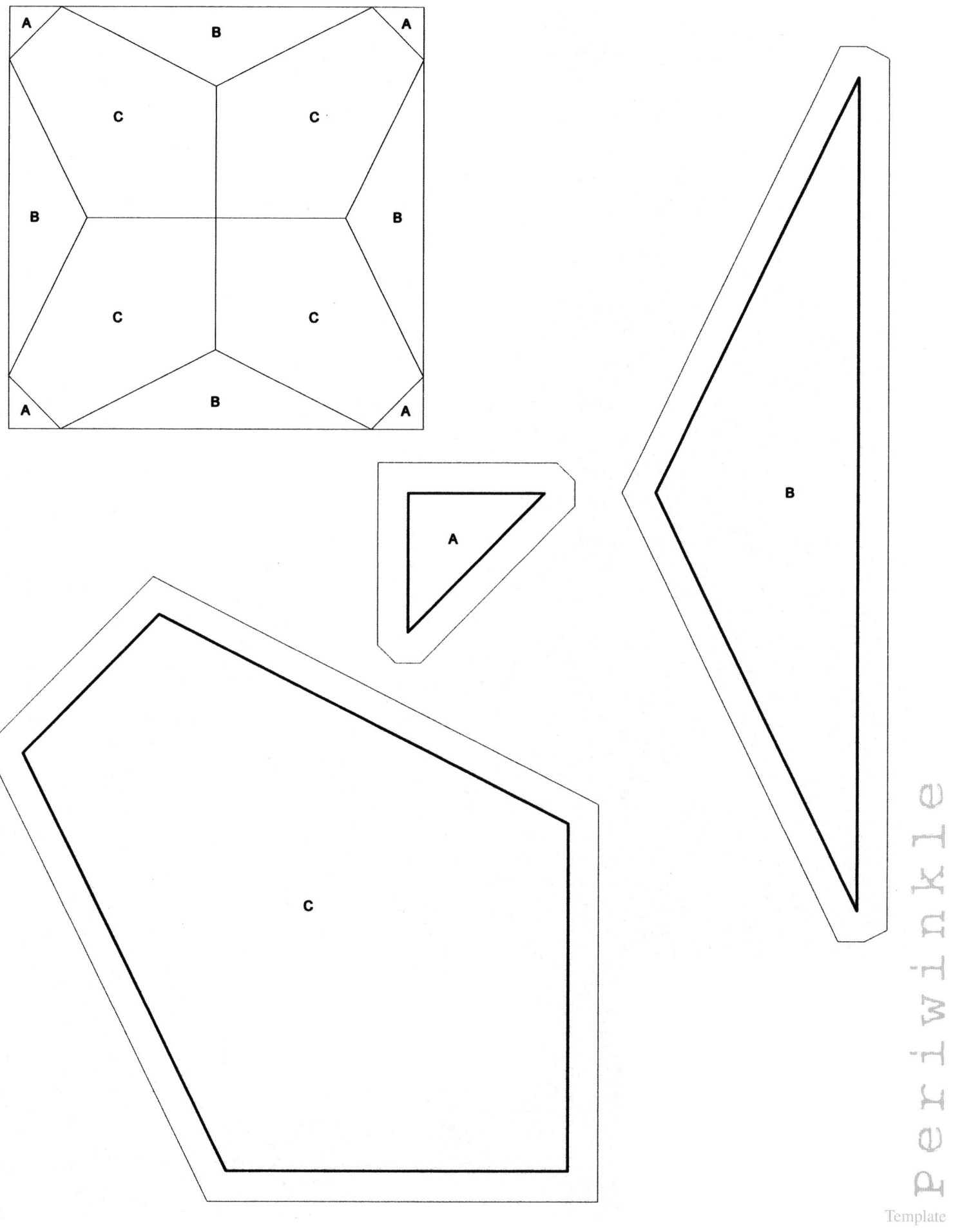

Periwinkle

Quilter's Fan

Block Size: 12" finished

Fabric Needed

Cream

Salmon or

scraps of your choice

We will use templates for this block due to the odd shape of the piece.

Cutting Directions

From the cream fabric, cut

32 pieces using template A

From the salmon fabric, cut

32 pieces using template A

To Make the Block

1 Sew a cream A piece to a salmon A piece. Make 32 pairs.

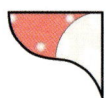

2 Sew 2 pairs together to make one unit as shown below.

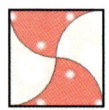

3 Sew 4 units together to make a row. Make 4.

4 Sew the 4 rows together to complete the block.

Quilter's Fan

From The Kansas City Star,

August 28, 1940:

No. 625

Original size – 5"

We suspect the creator of this design picked up a mental suggestion from the swirling blades of an electric fan. The pattern comes from Mrs. S. E. Axtell, Westphalia, Kas.

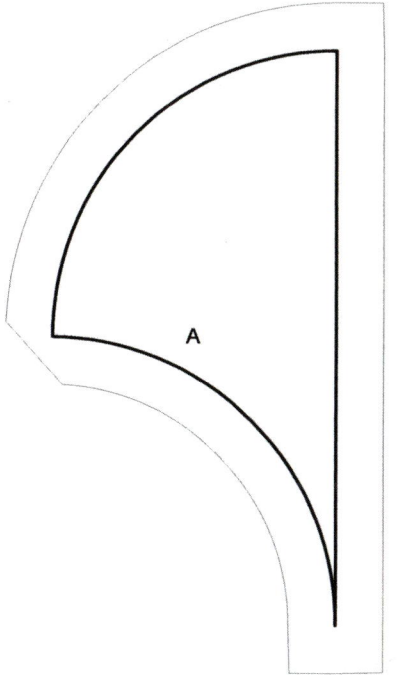

Bear's Paw

Block Size: 14" finished

Fabric Needed

Dark blue

Medium blue

Tan

This block can be made using rotary cutting directions.

Cutting Directions

From the dark blue fabric, cut

1 – 2 1/2" square (template A)

8 – 2 7/8" squares or 16 triangles using template B

From the medium blue fabric, cut

4 – 4 1/2" squares (template D)

From the tan fabric, cut

8 – 2 7/8" squares or 16 triangles using template B

4 – 2 1/2" squares (template A)

4 – 2 1/2" x 6 1/2" rectangles (template C)

First appeared in The Star **September 15, 1937**

To Make the Block

1 You will need to make 16 dark blue/tan half-square triangle units. To make the half-square triangles, draw a line from corner to corner on the reverse side of the tan 2 7/8" triangles. Place a tan square atop a dark blue square and sew 1/4" on either side of the drawn line. Using a rotary cutter, cut along the drawn line. Open each unit and press toward the darker fabric. If you cut your triangles separately, sew a dark blue B triangle to a tan B triangle.

2 Sew the half-square triangle units into pairs as shown. You need 4 units of each orientation.

3 Sew a pair of half-square triangles to the medium blue D squares as shown.

4 Sew a tan 2 1/2" A square to a pair of half-square triangles. Make 4 strips. Two of the strips will be mirror images of the others as shown below.

Bear's Paw

5 Sew a strip to the top of the B/half-square triangle unit. Make 4 of these corner units.

6 Sew a corner unit to either side of a tan C rectangle.

7 Sew a tan C rectangle to either side of the dark blue A square.

8 Sew the three rows together to complete the block.

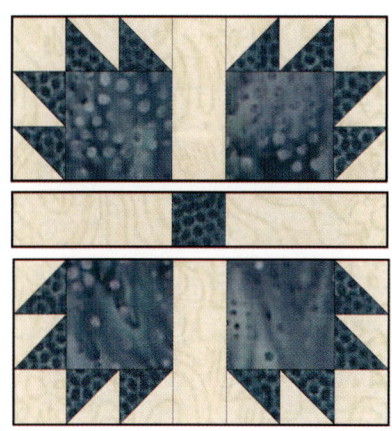

From The Kansas City Star,

September 15, 1937:

No. 520

Original size – 14"

This is a welcome pattern because it can be used to make small scraps into a lovely quilt.

Big Bear's Paw

From The Kansas City Star,

June 15, 1960:

No. 1050

Original size – 14"

Brown and white would be appropriate for developing the Big Bear's Paw, particularly the toes. The design comes from Amelia Lampton, Aguilar, Colo.

History of the Block

"My Bear Paws" stitched and quilted by Marilyn Becker, Wausau, Wis. Pattern from the book "QUILTS! QUILTS!! QUILTS!!! The Complete Guide To Quiltmaking" by Diana McClun and Laura Nownes, The Quilt Digest Press, San Francisco, USA, published 1988.

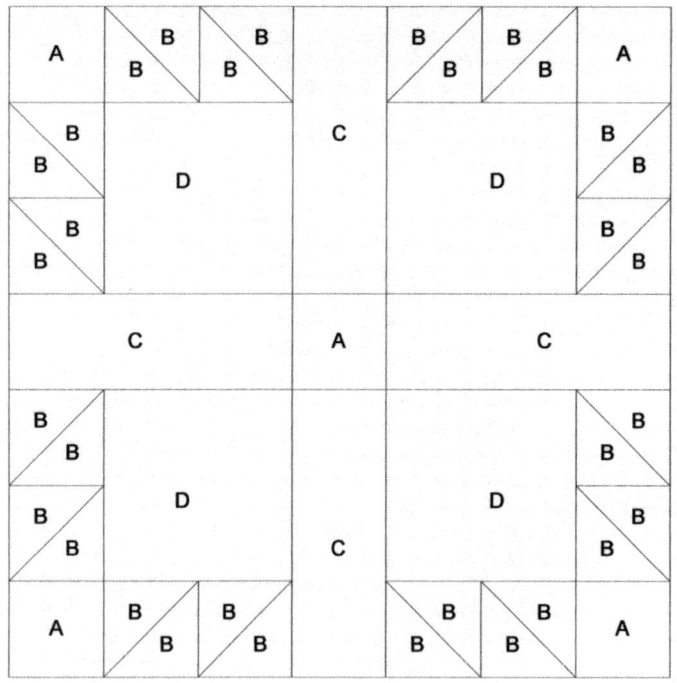

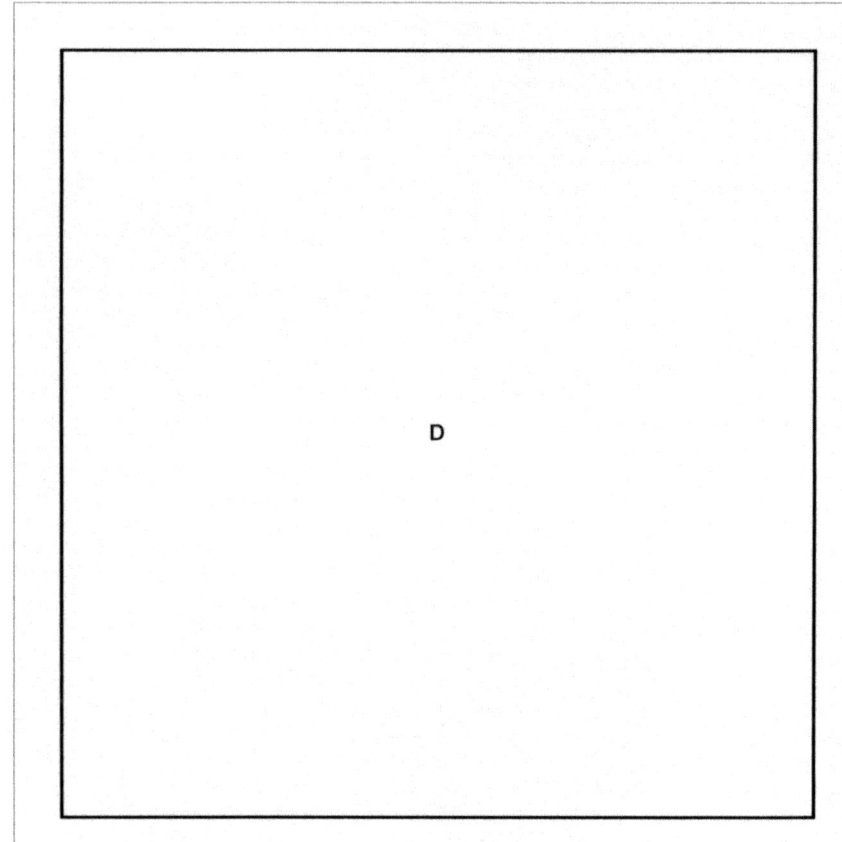

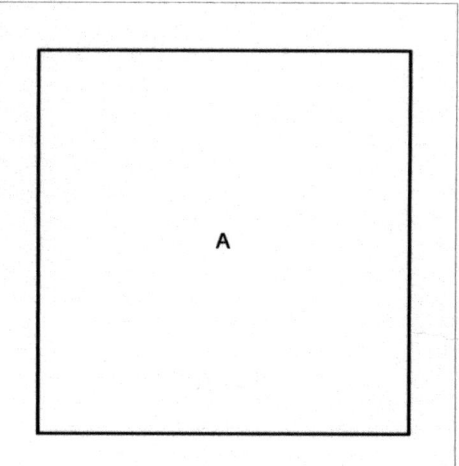

Bear's Paw

Template

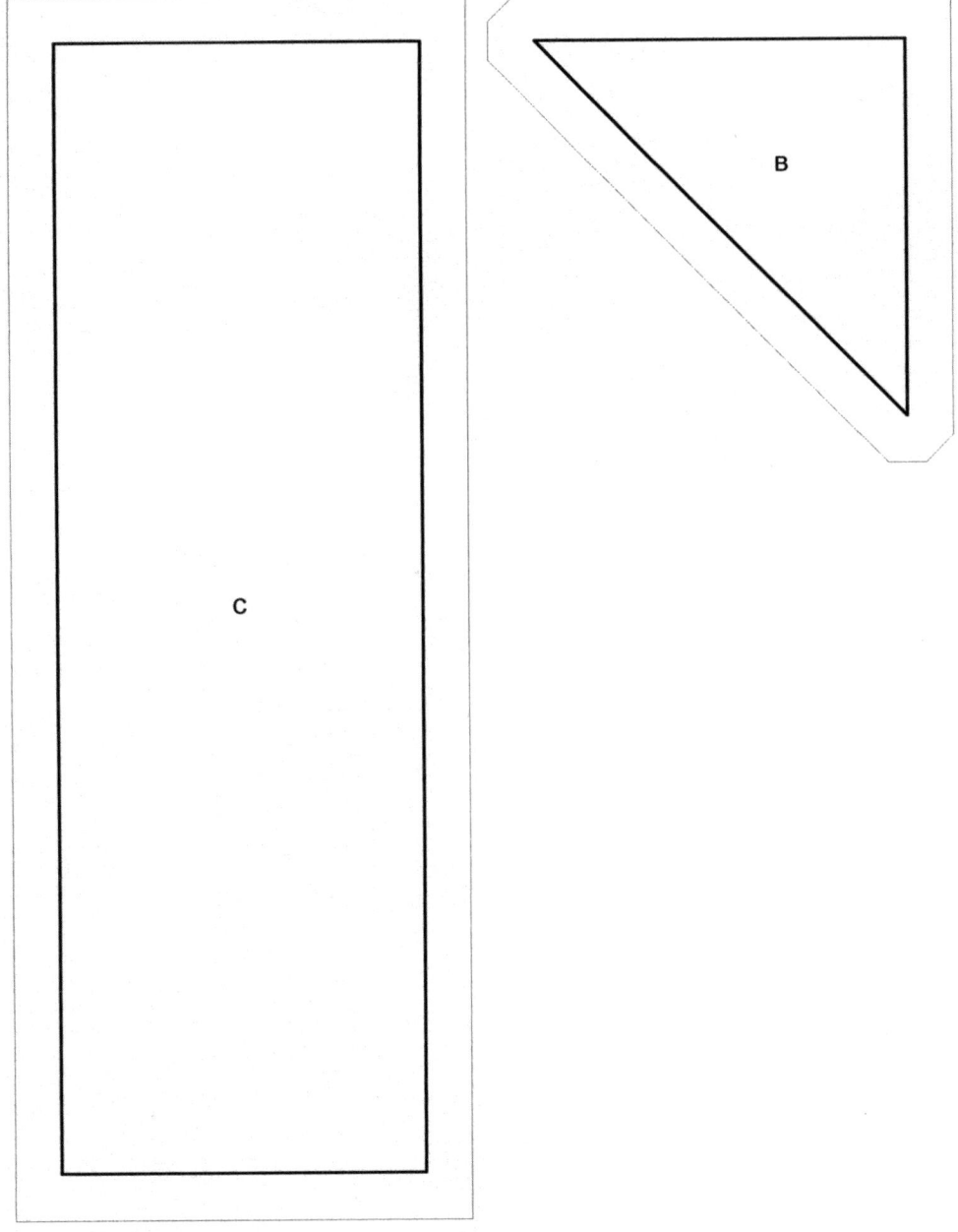

C

B

Bear's Paw

Appeared in The Star **February 22, 1950**

To Make the Block

1

NOTE: Use a scant 1/4" seam allowance when sewing.

You will need to make half-square triangle units for this block.

To make half-square triangles, draw a line from corner to corner on the diagonal on the reverse side of the lightest fabric. Place a light square atop a darker square and sew 1/4" on each side of the line. Use your rotary cutter and cut on the line. Open each unit and press toward the darkest fabric.

Make 4 dark red print/background half-square triangles, 8 dark red tone-on-tone/background half-square triangles and 4 shirting/dark red print half-square triangles.

Sew the squares and half-square triangles together into rows as shown below. You will need to make 5 rows.

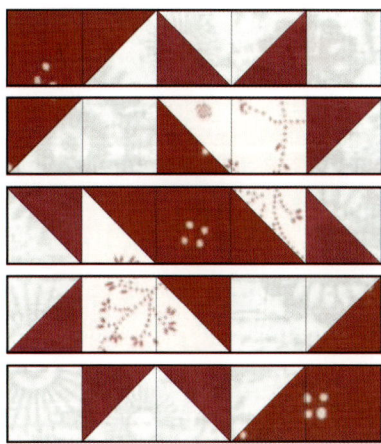

Queen Charlotte's Crown

Block Size: 12" finished

Fabric Needed

1 Dark red print

1 Tone-on-tone dark red

1 Red and white shirting

1 White for background

You can use rotary cutting directions for this block. If you choose to use templates, they are provided as well.

Cutting Instructions

From the white fabric, cut

4 – 2 7/8" squares (template A)

6 – 3 1/4" squares or 12 triangles using template B

From the dark red print, cut

3 – 2 7/8" squares (template A)

4 – 3 1/4" squares or 8 triangles using template B

From the tone-on-tone dark red, cut

4 – 3 1/4" squares or 8 triangles using template B

From the shirting fabric, cut

2 – 2 7/8" squares (template A)

2 – 3 1/4" squares or 4 triangles using template B

Queen Charlotte's Crown

From The Kansas City Star,

February 22, 1950:

No. 868

Original Size - 6".

Much of the effectiveness of this design is attained by choosing a small print in vivid colors for the triangular quilt blocks, and keeping the tips of the blocks sharp. The pattern comes from Mrs. Bertha Troutman, Ottumwa, Ia.

2 Sew the rows together to complete the block.

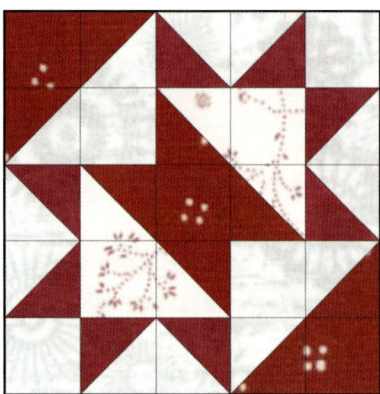

Press the seam allowances under on the outer edges of each of the leaves and pin in place. The center and point of each leaf should line up with the crease that goes toward each corner. Tuck the widest end of each leaf under the flower. Appliqué all in place.

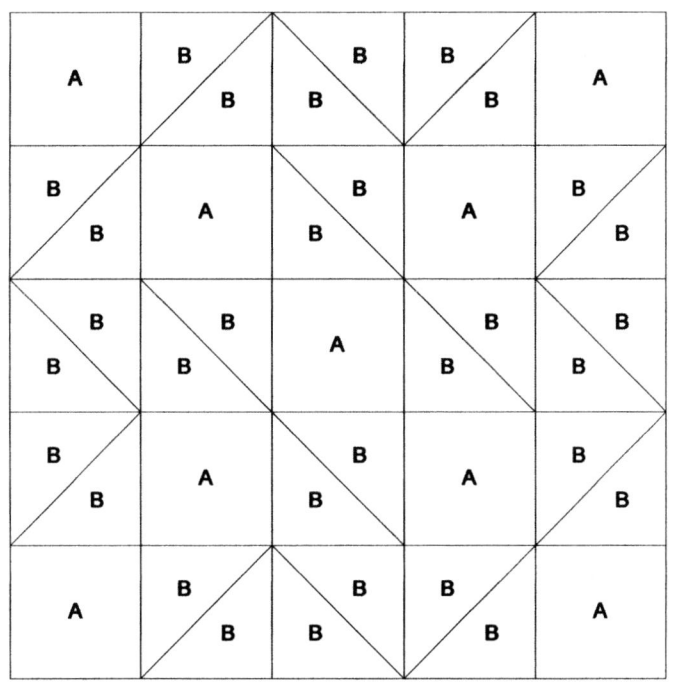

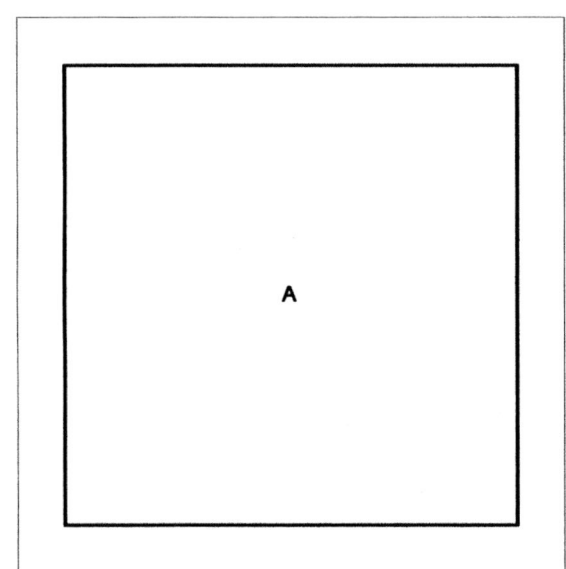

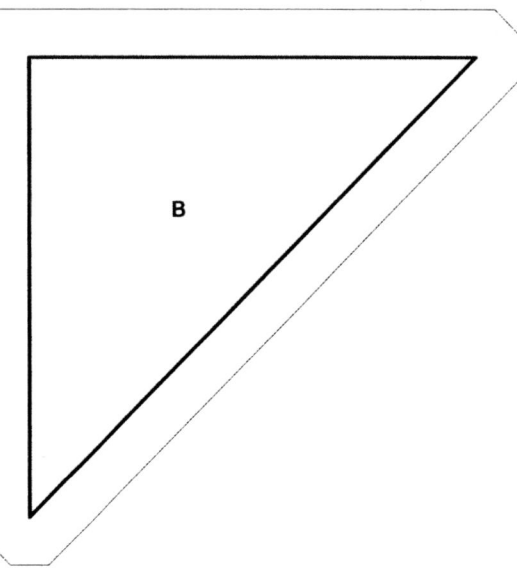

Template

Mountain Road

Block Size: 12" finished

Fabric Needed

Purple

Cream

We'll be using templates for this block because of the odd sizes and shapes of some of the pieces.

Cutting Instructions

From the cream fabric, cut

4 rectangles using template B

2 rectangles using template E

6 triangles using template C

From the purple fabric, cut

2 pieces using template D

1 piece using template F

6 squares using template A

To Make the Block

1 Sew a cream C triangle to either end of the D strip. Make two strips like this.

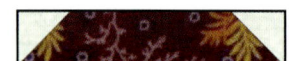

2 Sew a cream C triangle to either end of the F strip.

3 Sew an A square to the end of the E strip. Make 2.

4 Sew the five strips you have just made together as shown to create the center of the block.

Mountain Road

5

Sew a B strip to the right and left of the center.

6

Sew a purple A square to the ends of a B rectangle. Make two and sew one strip to the top of the block and one to the bottom.

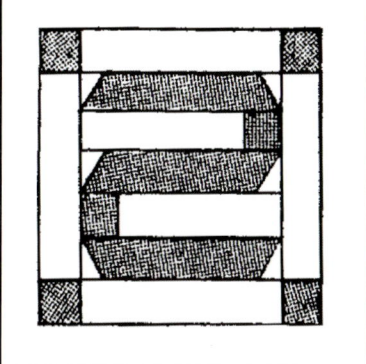

From The Kansas City Star, October 17, 1936:

No. 476

Original size – 9 1/4"
Developed in green and white or any other color combination you choose, this design makes a lovely quilt, whether set together as an allover pattern or spaced by strips of solid color.

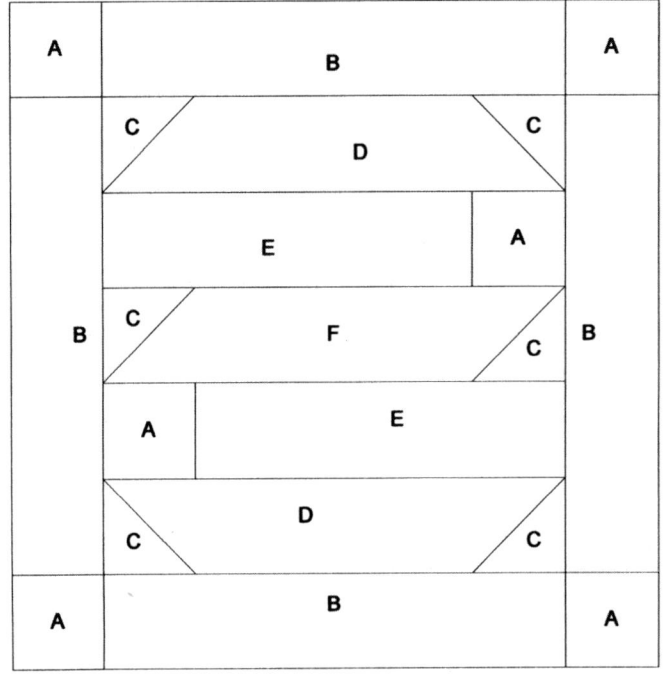

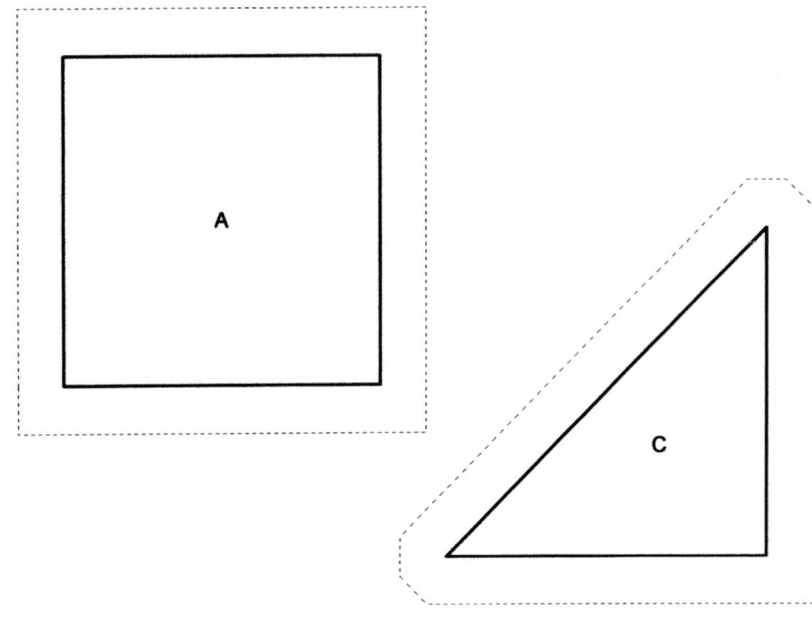

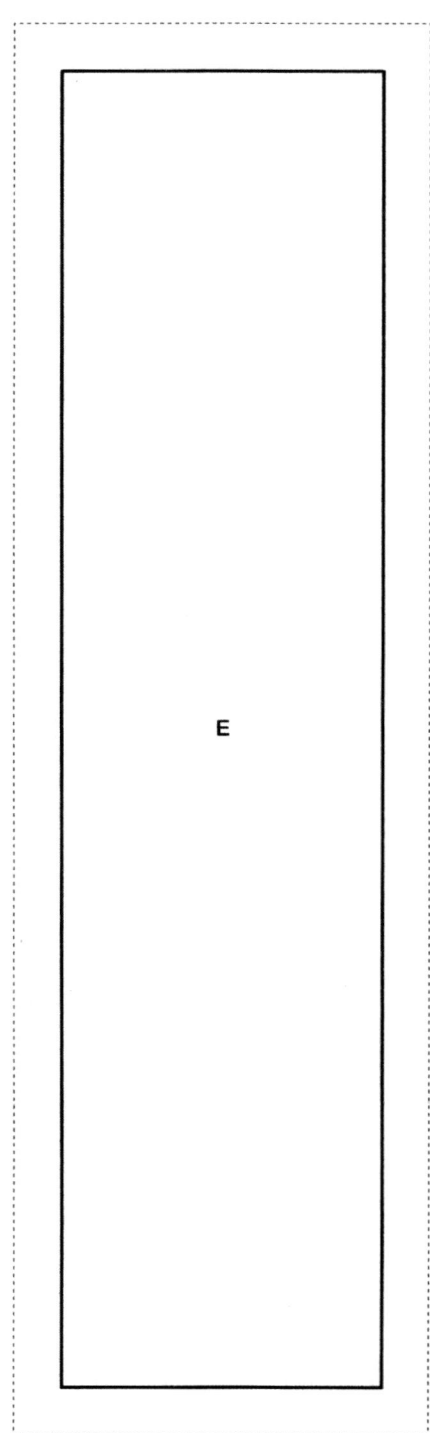

Mountain Road

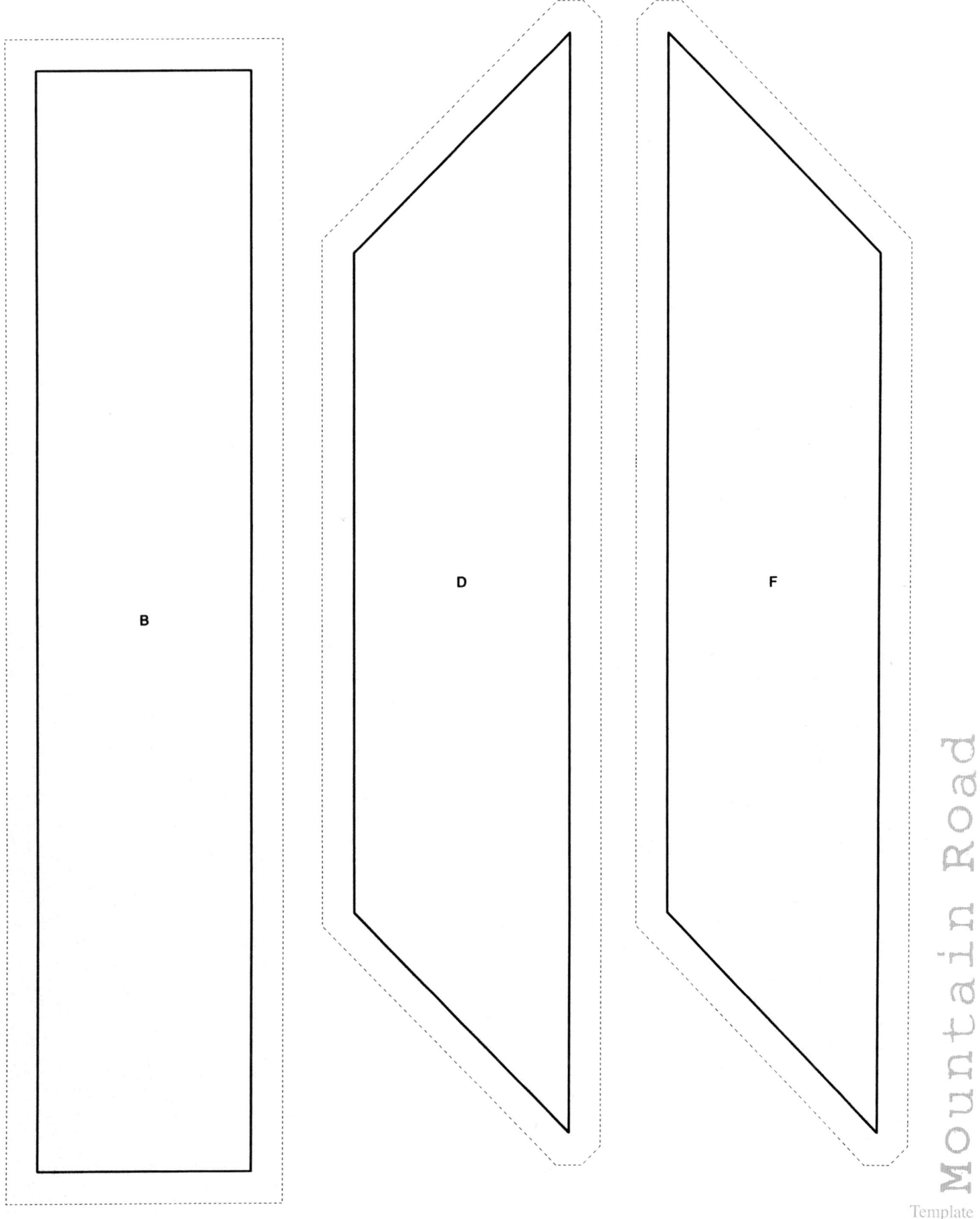

B

D

F

Mountain Road

Star of Alamo

Block Size: 9" finished

Fabric Needed

Brown

2 Cream

We'll make this block using templates.

Cutting Instructions

From the brown fabric, cut

4 pieces using template D

From the one of the cream fabrics, cut

4 pieces using template A

From the other cream fabric, cut

4 pieces using template B and

1 square using template C

To Make the Block

1

Sew a cream A piece to a brown D piece. Add a cream B piece. Make 4.

2

Stitch the A-D-B sections to the center C square. Stitch across the D-C seam line first, then close the seam between the A and B pieces.

Star of Alamo

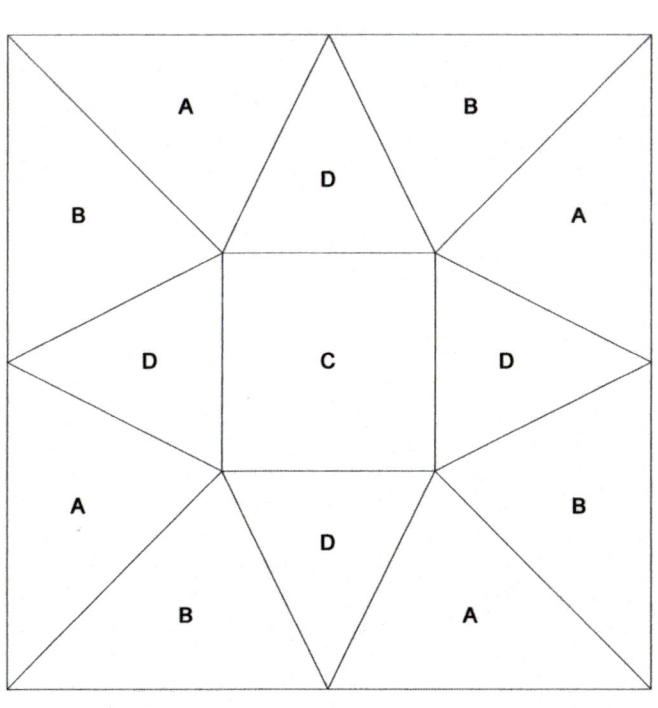

From The Kansas City Star,

November 12, 1941:

No. 666

Original size – 8 1/4"
A youthful masculine artist contributed this quilt block pattern.
He is E. P. Long, Jr., Bonnerdale, Ark., who named the design in honor of his school.

History of the Block

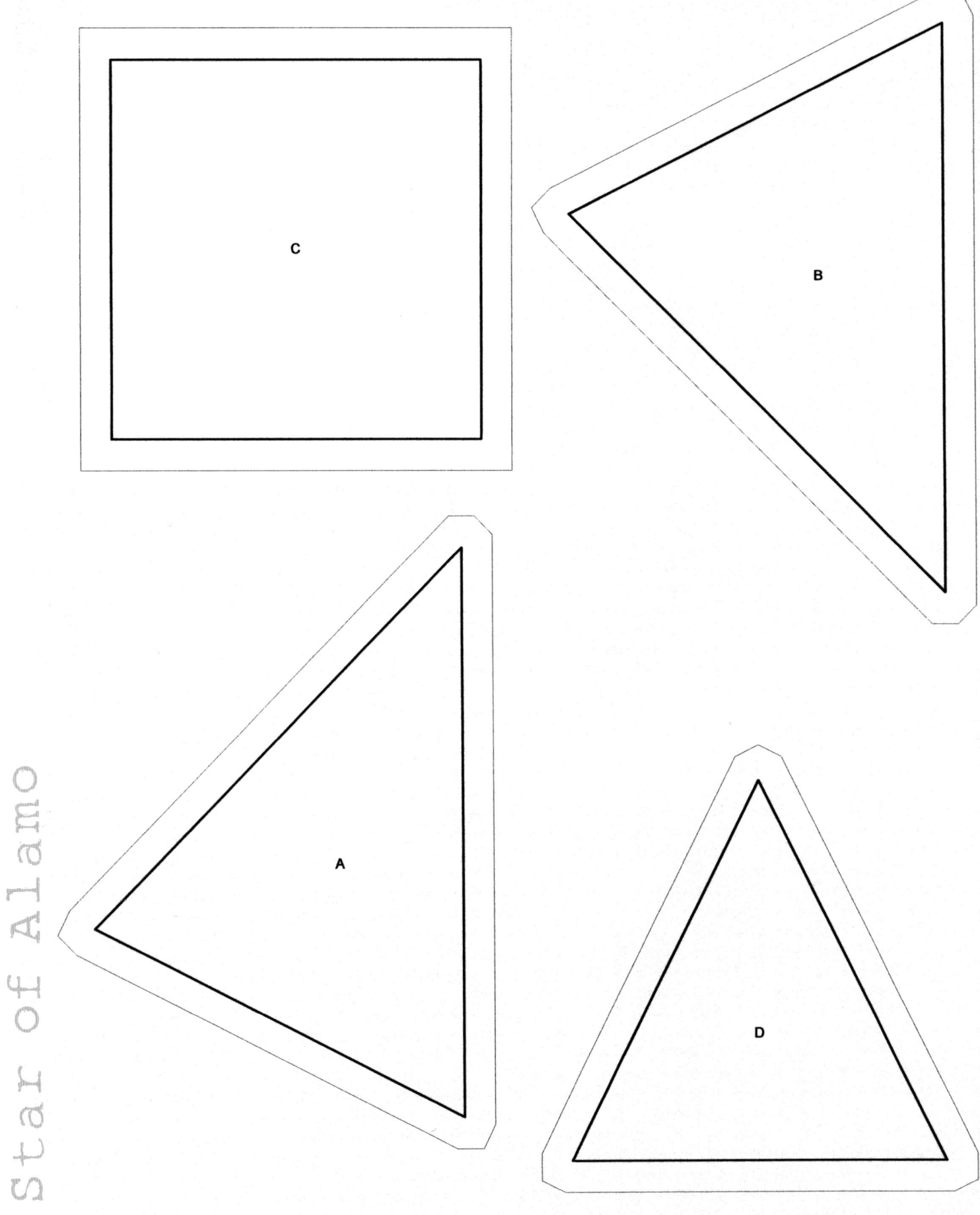

C

B

A

D

Star of Alamo

Template

Appeared in The Star **July 25, 1931**

Sugar Loaf

Block Size: 10" finished

Fabric Needed

Blue

Shirting

Light background print

You'll need to use templates for this block.

Cutting Instructions

From the blue fabric, cut

4 diamonds using template D

5 triangles using template C

From the shirting fabric, cut

6 diamonds using template D

From the background print, cut

1 triangle using template A

1 triangle using template B

To Make the Block

1
Sew the diamonds together into rows as shown below. Begin each row with a blue C triangle.

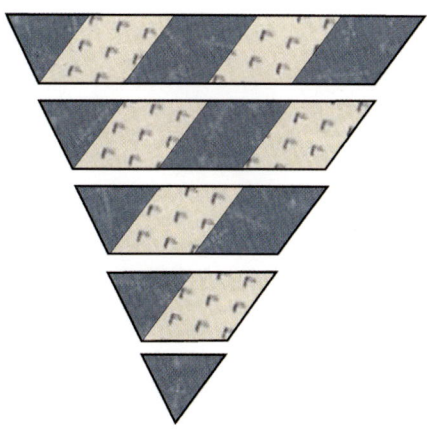

2
Sew the rows together to make one large triangle as shown.

From The Kansas City Star,
July 25, 1931:
No. 180

Original size - 12 1/2" high x 12 1/2" wide

A clever arrangement of diamonds and triangles is responsible for this interesting quilt pattern. It is not hard to piece either so it is an ideal pattern for work on hot summer days. It is pieced in rows, then set together as shown above in the section of the quilt. While this shows black and white there are many ways to use colors, either plain or otherwise. If prints are used, have each row of a different color with perhaps one row of solid color. Of course, there will be half blocks at the sides and ends. The block, itself shown in the center, is not an equilateral triangle. Cut an equal number of plain blocks and allow for seams.

3 Add the A and B triangles to either side of the triangle to complete the block.

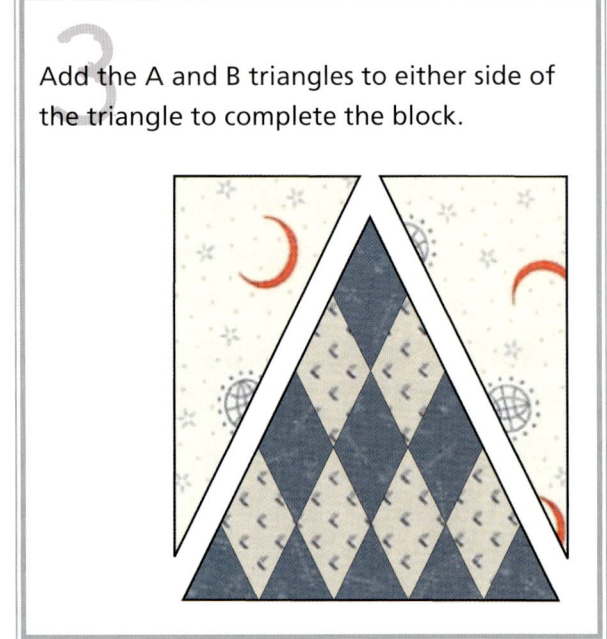

"Sugar Cone" stitched and quilted by Judy Boyle, Hudson, Ohio. Pattern inspired from the book "Childhood Treasures: Doll Quilts by and for Children" by Merikay Waldvogel, Good Books, published 2008.

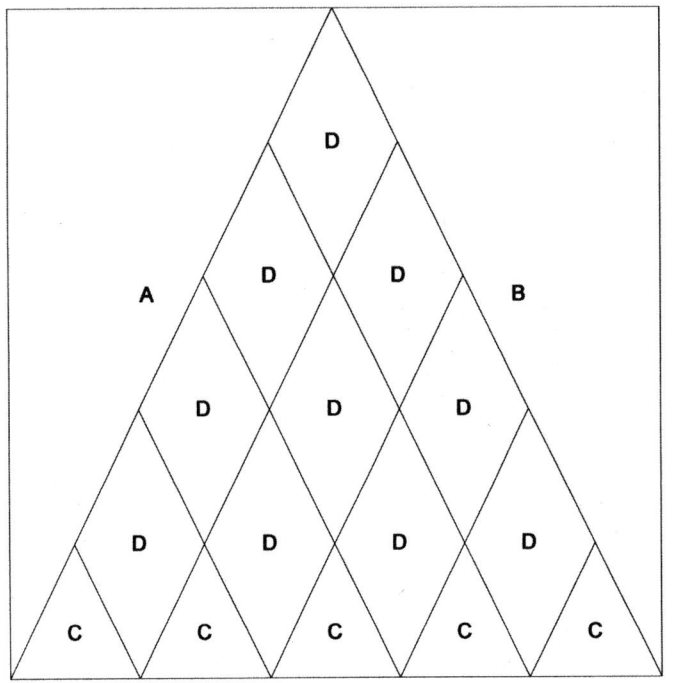

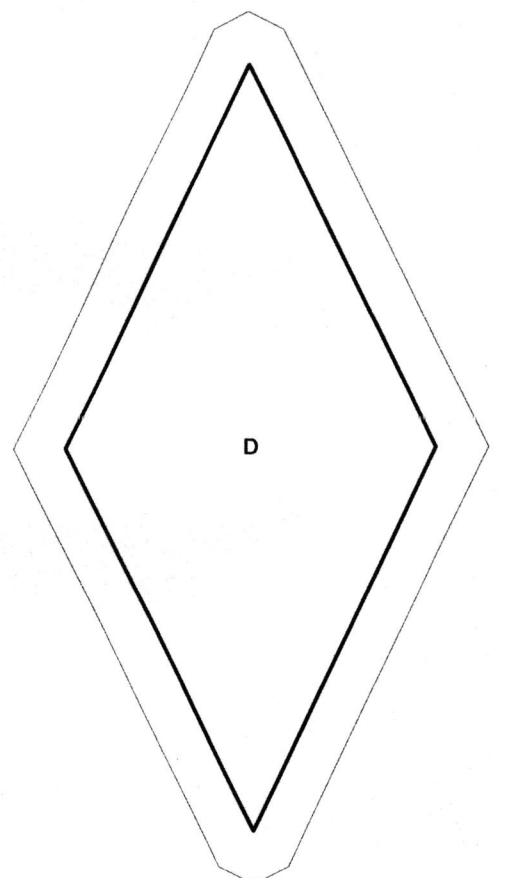

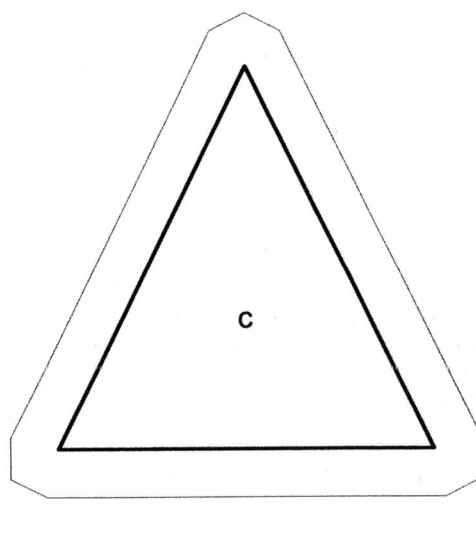

Sugar Loaf

Template

A

Sugar Loaf

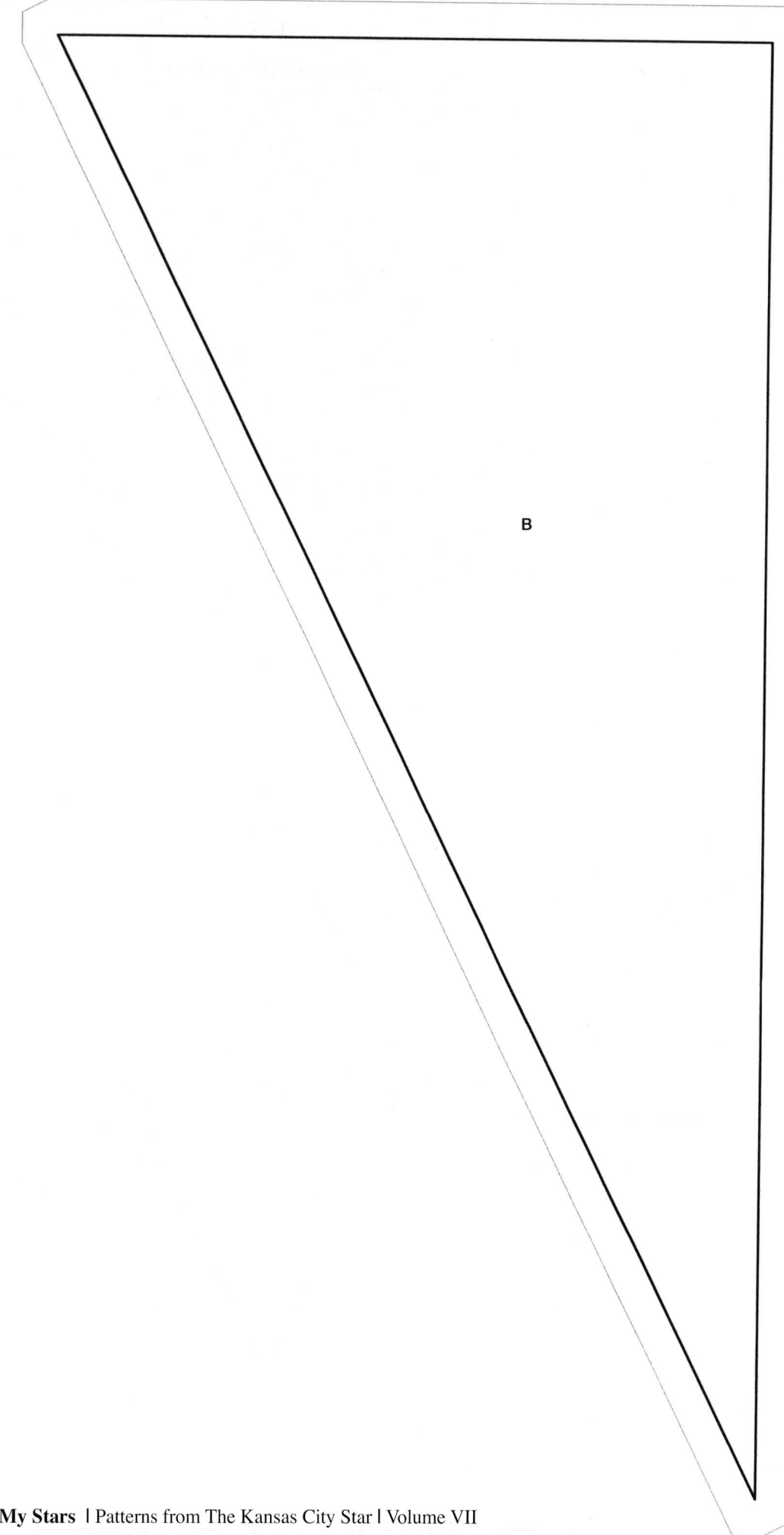

B

Appeared in The Star **July 23, 1941**

Quint Five

Block Size: 12" finished

Fabric Needed

Brown

Cream

To Make the Block

1 Sew a cream B triangle to either side of a brown A piece. Make 8 of these AB units.

2 Sew a brown A piece to either side of a C square as shown. Make 4 of these AC units.

 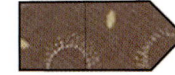

3 Sew an AB unit to either side of an AC unit. This makes one quadrant of the block. Make 4.

We'll make this block using templates.

Cutting Instructions

From the brown fabric, cut

16 pieces using template A

4 - 2 5/8" squares (template C)

From the cream fabric, cut

4 – 4 1/4" squares. Cut each square from corner to corner twice on the diagonal or cut 16 triangles using template B.

Quint Five

From The Kansas City Star,

July 23, 1941:

No. 653

Original Size - 12 1/2"

The name for this quilt block pattern was chosen by Mrs. Pearl Bacon, Achilles, Kas., in honor of the famous Dionne quintuplets of Canada.

4 Sew the 4 quadrants together to complete the block.

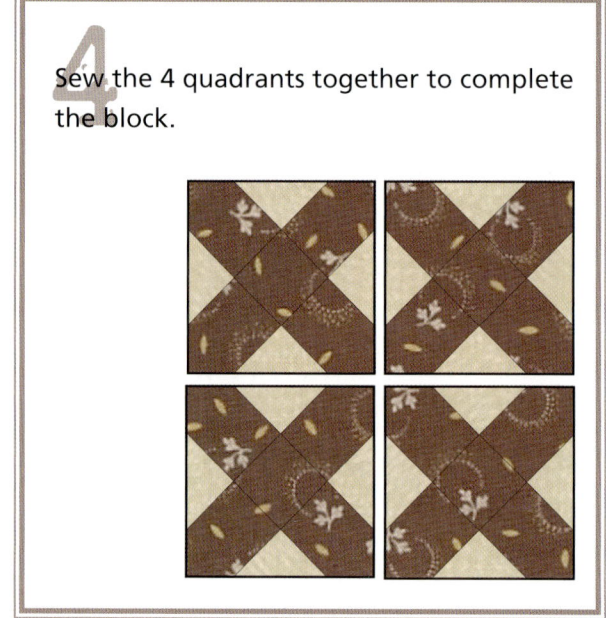

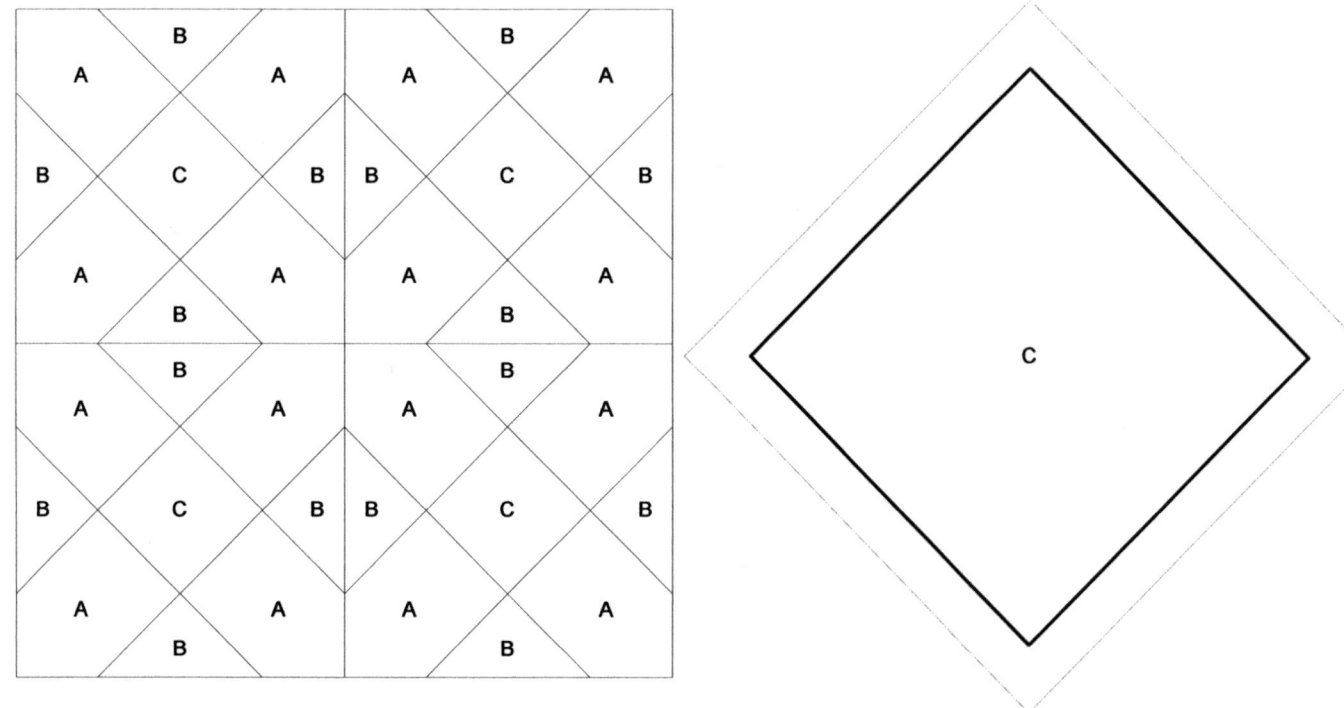

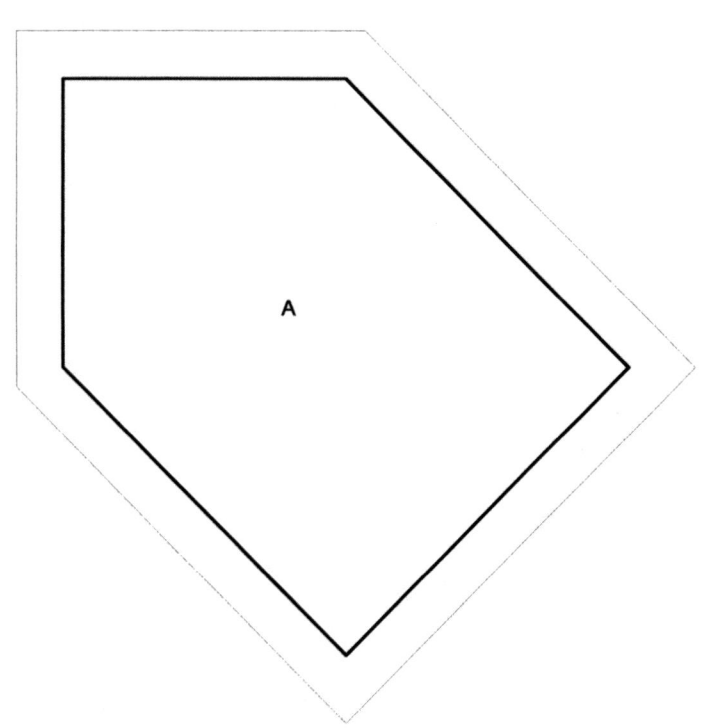

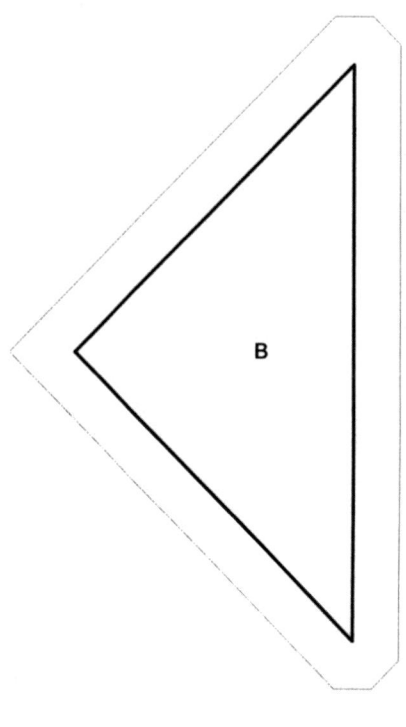